Business K731

TABLE OF CONTENTS
& ACKNOWLEDGEMENTS

PAGE

Richard Ivey School of Business

The University of Western Ontario

9B10D016

AMERICAN CONSTRUCTORS INC.: WORLD OUTREACH EXPANSION PROJECT

Leanne Miele wrote this case under the supervision of Professor Kenneth J. Klassen solely to provide material for class discussion. The authors do not intend to illustrate either effective or ineffective handling of a managerial situation. The authors may have disguised certain names and other identifying information to protect confidentiality.

Version: 2013-07-26

It was 8:00am on September 24, 2009. Tom Grott, senior project manager for American Constructors, Inc (ACI), sat down with his team to assess the progress on their current project at World Outreach Church (WOC) in Murfreesboro, Tennessee. That afternoon, Grott needed to meet with the architect and the client to report on the company's probability of completing the work by the project finish date, December 14, 2009; he also needed to discuss the close-out requirements with the architect. The impending deadline was creating significant tension on the site. Originally scheduled for March 2010, the date was pushed up to December as per the client's request in spring 2009. Initially they requested that the property be completed for use on the Thanksgiving holiday (November 26, 2009). Grott recognized the impossibility of their request and compromised by adding a few additional weeks to that date. He knew that the church was relying on him to have the project completed for the Christmas season.

WOC was established in 1980 as an inter-denominational Christian congregation. As of late 2009, the church had more than 5,000 members and was broadcast every Sunday morning on three different television channels. In addition to its television broadcasts, WOC offered a 24/7-radio show and MP3 downloads of selected sermons. The church had become a major establishment in middle Tennessee, with claim to several high-profile congregants. Grott's leadership on this project would leave an impression on the local and church communities. In an effort to uphold the reputation of ACI and protect future opportunities, Grott needed to ensure that the project was completed on time.

AMERICAN CONSTRUCTORS, INC.

ACI was founded in 1979, and by 2009 was enjoying the benefits of being one of the leading commercial construction companies in middle Tennessee. Since its inception, the company contracted more than 600 projects, totalling in excess of US$1 billion[1]. The company became licensed in 15 states across the United States. Some of its famous contracts included major Nashville landmarks such as The Country Music Hall

---

[1] *All monetary values in US$ unless otherwise stated.*

of Fame & Museum and The Schermerhorn Symphony Center (see Exhibit 1). The company also successfully contracted the construction of several music publishers' headquarters in the Nashville area, namely the American Society of Composers, Authors and Publishers (ASCAP), Sony-Tree and Electrical & Musical Industries, commonly known as EMI.

In the first 30 years of operations, the company worked hard to earn multiple awards, which recognized its dedicated staff and the calibre of its work. Some of these awards included multiple awards of excellence in development as well as awards in safety, safety training and evaluation processes. Although a drastic slump in the construction market in 1988 threatened the future of the firm, the ACI team worked diligently to keep the company alive. In 2009, ACI was a strong and growing firm with several projects across the state of Tennessee.

THE CHURCH CONSTRUCTION MARKET

ACI focused its contracts in five construction markets; public and private schools, churches, health care facilities, entertainment and office buildings/complex properties. The company's first church construction project came in the early 1990s. It was during this project that they met the firm's president as of 2009, Dan Brodbeck, as he was serving on the building committee for the church. Due greatly to the success of the project and the relationships forged during this time, Brodbeck was persuaded to join the ACI team. Throughout the 1990s, area churches continued to be a strong market for the company: it completed four more properties by 1996 and continued accepting major church expansion projects into the new millennium.

Construction of religious centres had been a booming industry across the United States. In 2006, the church construction market was estimated at more than $7.6 billion alone. The American Institute of Architects (AIA) released a forecast in 2009, predicting that the religious construction sector would experience higher growth than all other non-residential sectors in 2010[2], showing that despite a struggling market, church construction could provide jobs for construction firms such as ACI, making them a highly valuable client. The WOC expansion was initially budgeted as a $31 million project; however, changes in the architect's design and a few unforeseen events resulted in an increase to $34 million.

WORLD OUTREACH CHURCH EXPANSION PROJECT

With 20 years of experience in the construction industry and a bachelor's degree in construction management, Grott was one of the most skilled managers on the ACI staff. Although Grott anticipated that it would be challenging to please the client by meeting the December 14 deadline, he was confident in his team of administrative staff, his crew of 10 labourers (carpenters, finishers, cleaners and machine operators) and the 25 different subcontractors. Exhibit 2 shows some of the progress as of September 2009. It was crucial that the building be usable by the congregation for the Christmas season even if there was some minor work still ongoing. At the completion of the church expansion project, the architect would provide Grott a punch list of minor tasks that the architect and WOC believed needed to be completed before the property would officially be considered complete. As part of running through the punch list, ACI would also do a last run-through of the property to ensure quality. Grott's goal was to start this final task, the architect's punch list, by the project deadline on December 14. He estimated that the architect's punch list would require five to 10 days, depending on their demands, and he was hoping the tasks required could be done while the congregation started using the building.

---

[2] http://info.aia.org/aiarchitect/thisweek09/0116/0116n_consensus.cfm.

A critical part of any contractor's job is coordinating the close-out of a project. In preparation for his meeting with the architect that afternoon, Grott had prepared a memorandum outlining their close-out responsibilities (see Exhibit 3). The items listed needed to be completed and submitted immediately, and had to be received back before the fire marshal's inspection of the property, which in turn would happen before work on the architect's punch list (see further details below). Grott would submit his request to the architect that afternoon and expected the documents to be mailed to his office in no later than four weeks (20 days), but no earlier than two weeks. In terms of capital projects of this size, it is not uncommon for construction to remain active several months after close-out documents are prepared; however, as noted in the memo, the General Guarantee and Warranty and the Final Release of Lien (two other important documents) could not be signed until the architect's punch list was completed.

The General Guarantee and Warranty was a document submitted to WOC by ACI affirming that the work they performed was in accordance with the details outlined in the original contract (see Exhibit 4). This type of document was important for a job this large, as it granted the client, WOC, a full year to inspect and evaluate the workmanship of the property. It also relinquished any responsibilities for ACI after one year. Although preparing this document would not take much time and would not affect the construction schedule, getting it signed after the architect's punch list was completed would be an important step that could take somewhere between half a day to one day, since the WOC would undoubtedly want to look over the whole project carefully before signing. The Final Release of Lien was also a very important legal document (see Exhibit 5). It would be signed by each subcontractor to record that they received their money and performed their duties, indicating that they no longer had any financial interest in the property (this would not affect the construction schedule).

Remaining Construction

In discussing the current progress with his team, Grott identified three main sections of the property that remained unfinished as of September 24, 2009. These sections included the bookstore/café/kitchen, the lobby and the sanctuary.

Bookstore/Café/Kitchen

In planning the final stage of the bookstore/café/kitchen section, Grott explained that work was already in progress on framing, hanging and finishing the drywall. He predicted that it would take the subcontractor, Cage Drywall, at least 21 more days to complete the work (at most 23 days). Once it was finished, installing the hard tile and finishing the stone columns would be started. These tasks would take 10 days and five days, respectively. At the same time that the hard tile and stone columns were started, Bridget Brodbeck, the project coordinator, explained that she had scheduled Integrity Architectural Millwork to begin millwork on the bookstore, café and kitchen;[3] she estimated that they required 15 to 21 days to complete the work. Following the millwork, casework (installation of cabinetry) could begin. Brodbeck estimated further that they needed five days to complete this task. Installation of flooring would take 10 days and would begin after the casework was finished. Upon completion of the hard tile and stone columns, installation of the glass was scheduled to begin. Expected to take no more than three days, the glass installation included windows and glass slabs for the storefront. Grott and Brodbeck arranged for

---

[3] *Integrity Architectural Millwork is a company located in Nashville, TN that specializes in woodwork, including reception desks, architectural paneling and custom moldings. They are a reliable millwork firm that has been used by ACI in a number of other large projects.*

Charlie Irwin Painting to come in after the glasswork was completed. Painting this area of the church would take 10 days.

Once the painters and flooring installers vacated the area, Grott's crew of carpenters would begin installing the doors and associated hardware. Larry Hawker was the project superintendent who oversaw the work of the crew on the site; his 38 years of experience had taught him that this task time could vary greatly. Hawker explained to the team that if the received doors were of the correct requirements and no hardware was missing, the carpenters would require five days to install them in the bookstore/café/kitchen area; otherwise, reordering and matching hardware to each door could make the task take an additional two days. At maximum, Hawker expected that the doors and hardware could take eight days, factoring in all potential problems. While the carpenters were working on installing the doors, Brodbeck had scheduled mechanical, electrical and plumbing (M.E.P.) work to take place.[4] On the work breakdown schedule, Brodbeck pointed out that 10 days were allocated to the subcontractors for these jobs.

As with the other sections of the project, the bookstore/café/kitchen would be completed with a thorough cleanup and run-through of the company's own punch list created by Grott and Hawker. Cleanup and completing the tasks on the ACI punch list for the entire project would each take approximately four days, and could be done simultaneously, but only after all three major sections of the project were completed. These tasks would be followed by a fire marshal inspection, which could take up to five days for a property of this size. Only after the inspection could the architect's punch list begin. As internal inspections were conducted at various stages throughout the project, the inspection of ACI properties by the fire marshal had historically always passed.

Lobby

The lobby of the expanded church was two floors high. ACI was currently working on the reception area and the ceilings. Grott predicted that it would take 10 days to complete the reception area. Millwork was the major task that remained unfinished: the millwork task included work on the reception walls, counter, columns and rails. While the full 10 days could be spent on the walls and rails, the work on the reception counter would only take three days and was slotted to be done in parallel with the other millwork. Work on the hard ceiling was almost complete and would also take the next 15 days. At the same time as these two tasks, Cage Drywall was scheduled to install the drywall in the lobby. (Cage Drywall had enough employees and subcontractors that they could work on multiple sections of the church simultaneously. This was also true for all the other subcontractors.) Within the following 15 days, the subcontractor was expected to hang and finish the drywall. As the team continued to review the schedule, Brodbeck discussed the plans for painting the lobby. Following the above three tasks, the painters were scheduled to paint both the first and second floor of the lobby and were contracted to take five days.

Flooring, another major task required to complete the lobby, was scheduled to begin once the millwork at the counter was completed. A thin concrete layer had to be laid in areas where carpeting was going to be put in so that the carpet was the same height as the flooring. Hawker described the process to the team, indicating that the task times could vary from as little as five days to as much as eight days, considering that the crew's ability to lay the concrete depended on the weather conditions, since much of the preparation was done outside. The hard tile in the lobby would be laid following the completion of drywall installation: they expected this task to take five days. The work would be completed by a subcontractor.

---

[4] *The major subcontractors for these tasks included Roscoe Brown Heating & Cooling and S&W Electric.*

Once the crew had finished their work with the concrete insert at the carpeted areas, a treatment would be applied to the wood flooring materials to acclimatize the wood, and the flooring would be installed. This task would take 35 days, including 10 days allocated for the wood treatment. The 25-day installation could take up to three additional days if the material was not laid with precision. Hawker noted that this time could also be shortened if needed by employing the crew to work overtime and help the subcontractor. With incentive, the subcontractors could usually be persuaded to get the job done sooner. Hawker estimated that the installation could be crashed to 30 days. Carpeting of the first floor, the stairwell and the second floor of the lobby were scheduled to begin following installation of the wood flooring and the hard tile, and would take approximately nine days.

Grott continued the meeting by discussing the finishing tasks involved in the lobby construction. Once the drywall and hard ceilings were completed, the crews would switch to work on and finish the public restrooms: this was expected to take nine days. At the same time, installation of glass and hanging the chandeliers would be done and was expected to take three days. The glass panels would span the height of the first floor and create a bright space by serving as the front wall of the building. The ceiling tiles also needed to be installed, and Grott and Brodbeck explained to the team that Acoustical Ceiling Tile was scheduled to work for five days following the completion of painting. After the ceiling tiles, washrooms, flooring and carpeting were done, the last two steps in finishing the lobby would begin. Done in parallel with each other, the doors and hardware needed to be installed and the M.E.P. work completed. Each of these two tasks were expected to take approximately 10 days for the lobby area, but they could be done in tandem with each other and with similar work in other sections of the building. After this, the cleaning and ACI punch list could be started, as explained above.

Sanctuary

The sanctuary was a large auditorium with tiered seating and a balcony with additional seating: it was designed to be the largest section of the expansion and therefore required a great deal of work and detail. Upon completion, the sanctuary, with its auditorium seating and large stage, would be an impressive room with state-of-the-art multimedia capabilities and intricate millwork. On September 24, Cage Drywall was in the process of hanging and finishing the drywall in the sanctuary. At the time of the last report, the company estimated that it would take 16 additional days. For planning purposes, Grott divided the sanctuary into three main areas; the auditorium seating, the bowl and the terrace.

Work on the auditorium seating was in its final stages. The core drill for the rails would take an additional two days before it was complete. Once this was finished, the rails would be installed along with carpeting at the seats. Grott estimated that these tasks could take five and 15 days, respectively. Carpeting at the rails would take five days but could only be started once the rails were installed and the wood panelling, trim and stage work was completed, which would take 25 days and could be started following the installation of carpet in the seating area. Painting could occur once the concrete floor was stained, the stage steps were carpeted and the carpet at the seats was completed, and was estimated to be finished within 20 days. The final step in completing the risers was installing the seats: this required approximately 20 days, and would be started upon completion of the wood panelling, trim and stage flooring work and the seat installation in the bowl area.

Grott and his team used the term 'bowl' to refer to the sanctuary area that was flat; in other words, the area directly in front of the stage that did not include the sloped portion. Installation of the seats in this area was scheduled to begin immediately following completion of the drywall: it was expected to take 20 days. Some of the concrete floor in this area needed to be stained and would take five days to finish, but this could begin only after the wood stage steps were completed. The steps would be started after the core drill for the rails was completed and would also take five days. In parallel to staining the concrete floor, carpet installation in the other sections of the bowl area could begin. Grott expected the subcontractor to take approximately five days to install carpet at the stage steps, flats and aisles. In the sanctuary, the crew would install the doors and hardware when the painting, wood panelling, trim and stage flooring work were finished. Again, this task could take from five to eight days, as Hawker previously explained for the bookstore area.

The architect designed a terrace just outside of the sanctuary. The window surrounds of the terrace were already under construction on September 24, and would take approximately eight days to be completed. The next task, which would take seven days, was waterproofing the terrace. As Grott continued reviewing the tasks with his team, he indicated that insulation would take three days, and could be started after waterproofing the terrace. Hawker explained the work on the concrete deck and stairs on the terrace; following insulation, the crew would pour concrete for the deck. There was large variability in this task, as progress in laying concrete is affected by the weather conditions. He expected the crew to take anywhere from 5-10 days to complete the deck. The stairs could be poured after the deck was finished. Because they take more time and attention, the stairs were scheduled to take 10 days; however, Hawker's crew was known for their dedication and hard work, and could greatly reduce this time with overtime on weeknights and weekends. At the same time that the stairs were being poured, aluminum rails would be installed. The rails would take five days to complete. The final task for the terrace was completing the masonry on the stairs. Southern States Masonry Inc. was contracted to do all bricklaying work for the project, and as Brodbeck explained, they were scheduled to come in at completion of the concrete stairs and railings and were expected to take 10 days. Construction of the sanctuary would be officially finished at this time and would be followed, as with the other two sections, by cleaning and preparation of the ACI punch list.

DEVELOPING THE PLAN

Grott and the team were beginning to notice that without overtime work and incentives for the subcontractors to work faster, the project may not be completed on time. In addition, there was no room in the timeline for errors or mistakes, which would inevitably occur. Grott still had a few hours before he was planning to meet with the architects and the client; since he wanted to be confident in this meeting that the job would be done on time, he needed to work diligently to arrive at a solution. Grott excused everyone on the team except for Brodbeck and Hawker.

The team knew how important it was to have the expansion completed by December 14 if they were to maintain the reputation of ACI and preserve future opportunities for the company. They began to work on the currently proposed schedule, hoping to be able to bring good news to that afternoon's meeting.

Exhibit 1

THE SCHERMERHORN SYMPHONY CENTER

Source: Photo provided by The Schermerhorn Symphony Center.

THE COUNTRY MUSIC HALL OF FAME AND MUSEUM

Source: Photo provided by American Constructors Inc.

Exhibit 2

THE LOBBY OF WOC SEPTEMBER 2009

Source: Photo provided by American Constructors Inc.

FRONT OF WOC SEPTEMBER 2009

Source: Photo provided by American Constructors Inc.

Exhibit 3

MEMORANDUM

AMERICAN

CONSTRUCTORS   **A-381**
World Outreach Church
Close-Out

September 24, 2009

MEMORANDUM

To: *(Name)* — *(Company)*

From: Tom Grott — Senior Project Manager

Re: World Outreach Church — Murfreesboro

Subject: Project Close-Out Requirements

Attached please find a summary of all Close out Manuals, Operation Manuals, Warranties, Guarantees, As-builts, and other items required for close out of the World Outreach Church Project. While there are certain items, such as Final Release of Lien's, General Warranty/Guarantee's, that cannot be completed at this time, there are many items that can and should be prepared immediately and submitted. Examples of items needed immediately that are necessary for our final inspections are as follows:

1.   Flame Spread Ratings on all fabrics, carpets, VCT flooring, vinyl or rubber base, acoustical ceiling tile, etc.
2.   UL Ratings on fire dampers, fire caulk barriers, insulation, and other items.
3.   Field Use and/or As-built drawings for all trades, whose work is complete.

In addition, all operation and maintenance manuals and close out manuals for MP&E trades can be immediately prepared and submitted.

Please review the attached list carefully and begin this process immediately. These items are to be forwarded in *triplicate* to our field office located at *(Address)* no later than *(Date)*. If you have any further questions concerning this please feel free to contact me.

TG

Exhibit 4

GENERAL GUARANTEE AND WARRANTY

General Guarantee and Warranty

World Outreach Church
Murfreesboro, Tennessee 37128

Job No. A-381

We hereby guarantee that all work performed and all materials and equipment furnished under this contract are in accordance with the Contract Documents and are free from defects of equipment, materials, or design furnished, or workmanship performed by this Contractor or any of our Subcontractors or Suppliers at any tier.

In accordance with Article 12.2.2 of AIA Document A201, if within one (1) year after the date of Substantial Completion of the _____ work or designated portion thereof or within one (1) year after acceptance by the Owner of designated equipment or within such longer period of time as may be prescribed by law or by the terms of any applicable warranty required by the Contract Documents, any of our work is found to be defective or not in accordance with the Contract Documents, we shall correct it promptly after receipt of a written notice from the Owner or his agent to do so unless the Owner has previously given us written acceptance of such conditions.

Exhibit 5

FINAL RELEASE OF LIEN

American Constructors, Inc.
P.O. Box 120129
Nashville, TN 37212
Office: (615) 329-0123
Fax: (615) 320-7966

Final Release of Lien

RE: **World Outreach Church (A-381)**
1921 Old Salem Road
Murfreesboro, TN 37128

The undersigned is and has been a furnisher of labor and material and/or a subcontractor on the above described project with American Constructors, Inc. as the general contractor and World Outreach Church as the owner thereof.

The undersigned does hereby acknowledge receipt of all monies due or to become due him for the furnishing of labor and materials and/or under its subcontract, including extras and represent that he has fully and properly completed his subcontract and/or furnished the labor and materials as required of it.

The undersigned does further make oath that the below stated list of vendors of labor and material to the undersigned have been paid in full and the undersigned does covenant and agree to forever protect, defend, and hold harmless American Constructors, Inc. from all claims of any and all furnishers of labor and materials to the undersigned on the above described job.

Any warranty or maintenance in the subcontract between American Constructors, Inc. and the undersigned remains in full force effect.

9B09C005

BEIJING EAPS CONSULTING INC.

It was November 2007, and Mr. Zheng, the chief executive officer (CEO) of Beijing EAPs Consulting Inc. (BEC), was sitting in his office, thinking about the conversation he has just heard between two of his employees, Mr. Yang and Ms. Song. The two colleagues often collaborated on various projects, and the conversation that Mr. Zheng overheard took place at an internal training program. The purpose of the training was to discuss problems and improve communication among employees. During the self-reflection part of the training, Mr. Yang, who managed the training department, commented:

> I notice that, recently, Ms. Song does not communicate with me as frequently as she used to. I guess the reason is that sometimes I get upset due to work pressure. My voice grows louder, and my tone is not always pleasant when Ms. Song passes tasks on to my department. Ms. Song, I apologize for that. You know, I have to work on 10 projects at the same time.

Ms. Song, who was one of the two project managers, replied: "I am not blaming you for that. I respect you very much, and I understand you are very busy, but your behaviour does make me feel afraid of communicating with you. Sometimes, I would rather stay late in the company to work on the tasks that are meant to be passed to you."

The conversation reminded the CEO, Mr. Zheng, that recently Ms. Song had been asking him to pass training-related tasks to Mr. Yang and his subordinates even though, as a project manager, Ms. Song had the authority to assign tasks to other department managers, including Mr. Yang.

Mr. Zheng was not worried about the personal relationship between Ms. Song and Mr. Yang, which had always been positive. However, Mr. Zheng was concerned that there seemed to be some confusion over managerial responsibilities in BEC's current structure. He had heard employees complaining about receiving tasks from both their department managers *and* from project managers, a situation that often created conflicts in their task deadlines. As a result, employees were not sure how to prioritize these tasks. Another problem arose from the fact they were confused about who their direct supervisor was: was it the department manager or the project manager? Project and department managers were located on the same level of the BEC hierarchy, and they worked together on planning and conducting each project. This work relationship between the two kinds of managers confused the employees: Who had the power to make a final decision when there is disagreement? On the other side of that same coin, the project managers felt that they did not have enough authority to give direction to the departmental employees.

Since the project management structure had recently been adopted by BEC, neither the employees not the managers were familiar with its procedures. Even so, Mr. Zheng strongly believed that project management was the right approach for BEC. Since its adoption, he had seen an increase of BEC's business and profit. But he also wondered what he could do to improve the present structure and procedures in order to clarify work relationships and responsibilities for his managers and employees.

COMPANY BACKGROUND OF BEC

Founded in 2001, BEC was the first consulting company to provide employee assistance services in mainland China. Between 2001 and 2006, there were only six employees in BEC; this number increased to 20 by the end of 2007.

Employee assistant programs (EAPs) are employee benefit programs offered by many employers, typically in conjunction with a health insurance plan. EAPs are intended to help employees deal with personal problems that might adversely affect their work performance, health and well-being.[1] EAPs are widely used in North America, but their use is rare in China.

BEC'S CUSTOMERS AND SERVICE

Most employees in BEC had a bachelor's degree or a master's degree in psychology, which made BEC the leader in providing professional EAPs services in China. BEC's market share was also the highest in mainland China. The company provided EAPs to many customers, including multinational organizations operating in China, such as Siemens, Samsung and IBM, and Chinese organizations such as Lenovo, the China Development Bank and Guangdong Mobile. These customers came to BEC with a common purpose: to provide their employees with psychological assistance to reduce stress and increase job satisfaction.

A typical project at BEC included the following procedures:

1. *Conducting interviews to collect information*: At the beginning of each project, BEC would interview employees in the customer company to collect information on employee stress, such as the sources of stress and the behaviours that employees exhibit under stress.
2. *Delivering brochures*: BEC provided information brochures to its clients' employees. These brochures included some basic knowledge on stress management, an introduction to the employee assistant program, details of the EAP process at their own company, and instructions on how to seek help from BEC.
3. *Setting up a toll-free helpline*: BEC set up a toll-free helpline for their customers' employees who could then use it to access one-on-one psychological consulting. BEC guaranteed that these phone conversations were confidential, which allowed the employees to openly discuss their problems with counsellors. Over 40 counsellors worked at BEC, mostly as part-time employees, and made up of

---

[1] *http://en.wikipedia.org/wiki/Employee_assistance_programs, accessed January 29, 2009.*

undergraduate and graduate students who were majoring in psychology. Others were school counsellors or hospital psychologists.

4. *Providing on-site training sessions*: BEC also provided on-site training to its customers. Attendees at these on-site training sessions ranged from front-line employees to senior managers. The training also provided managers with stress management skills.

BEC'S STRATEGY CHANGE

In BEC's early years, its founders lacked business experience, so they sought out BEC's opportunities to conduct practical research into stress management practices. Therefore, in the first few years, the founders did not put much effort into increasing their customer numbers. By the end of 2006, however, when its business had rapidly increased, BEC began to change its strategy and structure. Mr. Zheng decided to shift the company's focus away from research to focus more on business practices and to tap into the market's potential profit sources.

This shift in company focus was influenced by BEC's successful business with Guangdong Mobile, a subsidiary of China Mobile (see Exhibit 1). In April 2006, BEC began to provide EAP services to Guangdong Mobile's branch in Guangzhou, which had more than 50 million customers across Guangdong Province, China, and more than 7,000 customer service employees.[2] On average, each call centre employee answered a customer inquiry every two minutes, covering questions about a wide range of Guangdong Mobile's products, such as phone rates, fees, policies and so forth. To provide high quality service to their customers, call centre employees had to memorize a wealth of information about Guangdong Mobile's products and services. In addition, dealing with customer complaints and with difficult customers was an ongoing part of customer service. Guangzhou Mobile faced high turnover rates and low employee satisfaction in its customer service department, and this situation eventually lead the company to contact BEC.

In 2006, Guangzhou Mobile signed a contract with BEC to provide its employees with psychological assistance, representing BEC's largest contract since the company had been founded. To provide faster and more direct service to Guangzhou Mobile, BEC set up an office in Guangzhou, the capital city of Guangdong Province, and regularly sent employees to the Guangzhou office. Guangzhou Mobile was very satisfied with BEC's service.

In January 2007, China Mobile, Guangzhou Mobile's parent company, sent a policy statement to its 31 subsidiaries across China, stating that each office must provide its employees with psychological assistance, and encouraging the provincial subsidiaries to pay more attention to their employees' psychological health. Immediately after that announcement, Beijing Mobile, another subsidiary of China Mobile, also came to BEC for EAPs service.

With its accumulated experience and increased business opportunities, BEC decided to put all of its limited resources into the company's current and potential customers in the mobile phone industry, a move that put a lot of pressure on the company's existing employees. Since all of BEC's employees were working on client projects, it was difficult to maintain the research stream that BEC had been working on. Due to the intense competition from the market at this stage, BEC had to focus on its business. BEC also had to face the realities of the labour market: the company needed employees with degrees in psychology, but only a

---

[2] *Source: http://campus.chinahr.com/2008/pages/gmcc/index.asp, accessed January 29, 2009.*

few universities in Beijing provided such degrees. The difficulty of finding qualified employees restricted BEC's growth and forced BEC's current employees to become team players and multi-taskers.

EAP was an emerging industry in China, which meant there was great opportunity accompanied by great competition. To take advantage of such an opportunity, BEC was going to have to make some changes.

BEC'S STRUCTURAL CHANGE

Faced with an increase in business volume and the resulting workload, Mr. Zheng felt that his company would need more people and a different structure in order to maximize the efficiency of BEC's human resources.

BEC's Structure Before 2006

Before 2006, there was no clear structure at BEC. Six full-time employees, including the two co-founders as managers, worked in a single office in Beijing. One of the co-founders of BEC was a professor of psychology at a university in Beijing, and most of the employees at BEC were recent graduates of that same university. BEC also hired many graduate and undergraduate students from the psychology department as part-time counsellors, whose main responsibilities were to provide psychological assistance through the company's toll-free helpline.

Before 2006, there were no clearly identified departments in BEC, and the full-time employees' job responsibilities were not clearly designated. Whenever there was a project, all BEC employees got involved. Usually, the managers would assign tasks based on each employee's skills and schedules. All employees worked on two or more tasks, including designing the project plans, interviewing customer employees, providing telephone and face-to-face consulting, designing promotional brochures, and so on. Employees treated these projects as more than just a job; they looked on each one as a learning opportunity. Throughout their work on a given project, BEC employees discussed the difficulties they had experienced and provided each other with suggestions for improvement.

At this stage, the informal structure worked quite well at BEC. The work process was mainly project-based, and all six members worked as a team on every project. Each employee's role and responsibilities were flexible and mainly depended on the employee's personal interests and schedule. This structure also allowed all employees access to all the stages of an EAP project, which helped them to learn new technology and understand each other's work. The small size and flexible structure of the company made BEC able to tailor its services to adapt to a variety of customer requirements. After each project, BEC would hold an internal workshop where employees would have an open discussion about the project: what they did well, what they needed to improve, what they had learned, and what they could expect from each other in the future. This flexible structure made BEC a learning-oriented organization with an open culture.

BEC's Employees and Structure Since 2006

In October 2006, faced with an increase in business from China Mobile subsidiaries and from other companies, BEC started to recruit more employees and set up new departments as a way of specializing its employees' responsibilities. The new structure included a marketing department, a consulting department, a training department, a research and development (R&D) department, an administration department and two project departments. Having two project departments would reduce the number of projects for each of the project departments so that the project managers would not face too many scheduling conflicts. The functions of the two project departments were very similar. See Exhibits 2 and 3 for BEC's organizational chart and a list of departmental responsibilities.

The top management team included a chief consultant, CEO Mr. Zheng, and a vice-president (who joined BEC in 2006). They each managed different departments, according to their own areas of expertise. The chief consultant led the R&D department because he was a university professor and because he had the most knowledge in EAPs research. CEO Mr. Zheng led the consulting and training departments since he was very familiar with these tasks. The vice-president brought a wealth of experience to his role as the leader of the marketing department. Since the two project departments had similar responsibilities, the vice-president and the CEO lead project departments A and B respectively, which gave both of them sufficient time to manage the projects.

Ms. Song managed project department B, and Mr. Yang managed the training department; both of them reported to Mr. Zheng. Ms. Song had a master's degree in psychology and had been a licensed psychological counselor in a local hospital before she joined BEC in 2004. Since 2006, when BEC started its new project management structure, Ms. Song had led many projects. Mr. Yang had worked as a professional manager in training industry for over a decade before he joined BEC in 2005.

In 2006, BEC decided to adopt a project management approach. For each project, a project manager would lead a project team. Teams would be composed of employees from marketing, consulting, training, and R&D. Together, project managers and other department managers would work out a plan for each project and would then co-conduct the plan. Project managers could assign tasks to other department managers and their employees, and department managers were free to ask project managers to adjust work procedures, based on the actual processes of each department. This new structure allowed employees to focus on their specialized fields and to grow more familiar with certain work procedures. For example, employees in the training department could spend more time on designing and delivering training sessions and less time on discussing contract content. Once the new structure was established, it saved a lot of time with respect to work assignments and preparation.

Mr. Zheng felt that BEC was much more efficient after the structural change. By March 2007, the number of employees had increased to 20, and Mr. Zheng was planning to hire even more.

SPECIFIC PROBLEMS

After the restructuring, Mr. Zheng felt that the company was more efficient and more market-oriented. He could see BEC growing rapidly, both in size and in profit in the near future. However, as BEC and its profits were growing, some problems began to surface. Since there were many projects going on at the same time, employees had to work on multiple tasks and face various demands from each project as well as meeting the day-to-day requirements of their own departments. Some employees were working on more than 10 tasks at the same time, many of which had strict deadlines. Employees had to carefully plan their schedules and work extra hours to meet all the deadlines. Moreover, sometimes tasks were urgent. For example, a customer would ask for an extra report or analysis, and BEC would try to meet this request, which meant that BEC employees would often have to fit a new task into their already tight timetable. It was very common for staff to work nights and weekends at BEC, just like the employees in many other organizations in Beijing.

Another problem at BEC stemmed from the project management system itself. The role of the project managers did not seem to be well accepted among the departmental staff. With two project management departments and five other functional departments, employees working on a project would receive directions from their department manager and from the project managers as well. When there was conflict between two managers' assignments, employees tended to use their own judgment to decide the priority of tasks and would then adjust their schedules according to their decision. On the other side of the fence, project managers felt frustrated by their relationships with managers and employees in the functional departments. Sometimes the project managers would feel uncomfortable assigning tasks to functional managers who were at the same level in the organizational hierarchy. According to the new structure, project managers and department managers were peers, so it was difficult to apply any direct influence on each other. And when the project managers did assign tasks directly to employees in these functional departments, they might find that the employees were already working on tasks assigned by their department manger and would therefore find it hard to make time for the project manager's task.

In general, BEC continued to experience problems with its rapid growth; the increase in business has certainly yielded an increase in profits, but these have been accompanied by several new challenges for management. Mr. Zheng planned to recruit more employees in the near future, but first he had to make sure that BEC's organizational structure and management processes were efficient and effective. He was not sure how he could continue to expand the company and solve the growing management problems at the same time.

Exhibit 1

CHINA: LOCATION OF BEIJING AND GUANGDONG PROVINCES

China Mobile: Officially established on April 20, 2000, China Mobile Communications Corporation ("China Mobile" for short) has a registered capital of RMB51.8 billion assets of more than RMB400 billion. It wholly owns subsidiaries in 31 provinces across China. The total number of customers had exceeded 240 million by the end of 2005. [1]

Map of China and the Location of Beijing and Guangdong Provinces[2]

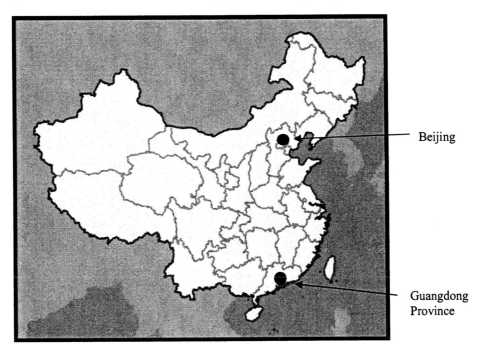

[1] http://www.chinamobile.com/en/mainland/about/profile.html, accessed January 29, 2009.
[2] http://commons.wikimedia.org/wiki/File:China_blank_map.svg, accessed January 29, 2009.

Exhibit 2

BEC'S ORGANIZATIONAL STRUCTURE IN MARCH 2007[1]

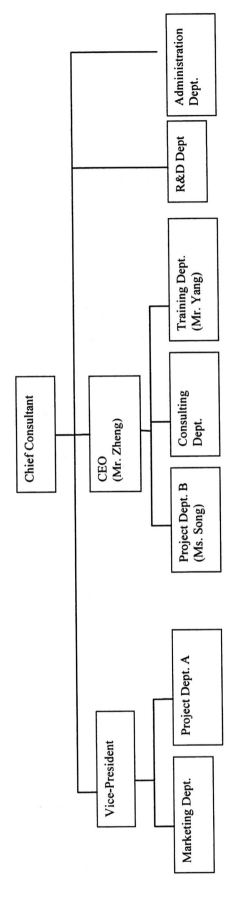

[1] Internal documents from Beijing EAPs

20

Exhibit 3

DEPARTMENTAL RESPONSIBILITIES[1]

1. Marketing Department:
   - Sell BEC's products and service to target markets
   - Establish BEC's leading image in the market
   - Promote BEC's brand name
   - Manage relationships with media, industry associations and partners

2. Project Departments A & B:
   - Co-operate with the marketing department to provide proposals to customers during the initial contacts
   - Allocate employees and other resources to provide high quality service to customers
   - Provide project documents to the R&D department; share the knowledge and technology created during each project with other departments
   - Research information related to the customer companies to develop a better understanding of the customers
   - Write advertising articles and co-ordinate with the marketing department

3. Consulting Department:
   - Develop and conduct a quality management system for consulting
   - Based on the requirements of the company, organize consulting teams through internal promotion and external contact
   - Provide consulting services to the customers based on the project department's design

4. Training Department:
   - Design and develop training courses on psychological assistance for clients' employees
   - Customize training sessions for various customers
   - Initiate employee assistant programs within customer organizations
   - Develop books and other publications on EAP

5. Research and Development Department:
   - Develop and conduct BEC's research strategy; ensure BEC's leadership in technology, products and services
   - Co-ordinate with other departments to develop new products
   - Collaborate with external resources (such as universities) on R&D issues
   - Design a project management process; design a research plan, data analysis process and report templates; provide training to relevant employees
   - Manage project documents
   - Co-operate with project departments to write the research plan, analyze data and write research reports

6. Administrative Department:
   - Conduct financial functions
   - Develop a human resources plan; develop reward and compensation systems; recruit new employees
   - Conduct daily administration functions

---

[1] *Internal documents from Beijing EAPs*

9B13C025

KEN PRIVATE LIMITED: DIGITIZATION PROJECT

Late one evening in August 2004, Saiyumn Savarker, chief operating officer (COO) of Ken Private Limited (Ken), was sitting alone in his corporate office. While he gazed at the panoramic view from his workplace in the Philippines, his thoughts raced to the vexing problems encountered in the first phase of the Genesis Digitization Project.

The Genesis Digitization Project required Ken to create digital archives of an American daily newspaper, *The Genesis Times*,[1] for its client, Dogma International. The coverage of this newspaper spanned 150 years. Ken had begun the project in April 2004 and had promised 10 years of digitized newspaper to the client by the end of July 2004. Unfortunately, Ken could not meet this deadline, and the delay did not sit well with Dogma International, since it had, in turn, already made a commitment to its customers. Infuriated by the delay, Dogma International sent out a dire warning: If Ken was unable to honour the commitment, Dogma International would not hesitate to cancel the project.

The project was in a state of flux. Ken had to deliver 35 years of digitized newspapers with enhanced image quality to Dogma International in a time frame of just two months. Moreover, cross-cultural context exacerbated Ken's problems and presented Savarker with a tough business issue. The gravity of the situation forced him to call an emergency meeting with the various managers of the Genesis Digitization Project to discuss and develop an action plan for successful execution and on-time delivery of the project to the client.

COMPANY BACKGROUND

Ken Private Limited

Ken Private Limited was established in March 1991 in Texas, United States, and was in the business of providing knowledge outsourcing and technology services. The firm helped its clients to use information efficiently as well as cost-effectively. The outsourcing content services of the company focused on fabrication services and knowledge services. Included in Ken's fabrication services were processes such

---

[1] *The name of the newspaper has been disguised to protect confidentiality.*

as digitization, XML and mark-up services, imaging, data conversion, content creation services and language translation services. Knowledge services, on the other hand, included content enhancement, vocabulary development, taxonomy, hyperlinking mark-up, indexing and abstracting and other general editorial services. The technology services focused on the design, implementation, integration and deployment of systems to author, manage and distribute content. By 2004, Ken had earned a great reputation in the market for its excellent performance. It had established offices in America, Europe and Asia, employing more than 5,000 employees, and its net profit in 2004 amounted to $90 million. Ken was one of the best market players in the industry, having earned many accolades for its superior performance, and its client base included many of the world's pre-eminent information, media and publishing companies, as well as leading enterprises in information-intensive industries.

Dogma International

Dogma International was a leading global content-publishing company, located in Michigan, United States. The company's history spanned 55 years, and its reputation in the market was based on the high quality and excellence of its services. The company developed information databases through multiple sources like newspapers, magazines, journals and from the works of thousands of publishers, in turn making the information available to customers through a web-based online information system. Large organizations and individuals alike depended on Dogma International to provide reliable and trustworthy information.

Dogma International acquired the rights to the microfilm archives of *The Genesis Times,* one of the most prestigious newspapers in America. The company considered it advantageous to shift from microfilm to a web-based product and decided to digitize the newspaper. For Dogma International, this decision represented a key strategic move as well as a prestigious project — to make available over the web millions of pages currently on microfilm, dating as far back as the 18th century.

As a part of this project, Dogma International aimed to convert the microfilm archives of the newspaper into a comprehensive digital archive. The main goal of the project was to make the content available and accessible, from anywhere in the world, to scholars, researchers, students, teachers, libraries and others needing the information. Every issue was to be digitized from cover to cover in an easily searchable, user-friendly format. Thus, the company sought to provide the information in both text-only format and full-page format so that users could view the information as originally published. The company also planned to index every issue thoroughly in order to enhance the browsing experience of the user, an effort that would require additional features, such as the ability to narrow searches (by date, author's name, keyword, etc.), view brief abstracts, and access each page with a user-friendly URL. Dogma International approached Ken to take on this task.

STRATEGIC AGREEMENT: DIGITIZING 150 YEARS OF HISTORY

On March 21, 2004, Ken entered into an agreement with Dogma International to provide its services for the Digitization Project, creating a digital historical archive of full runs of *The Genesis Times.* Under the agreement, Ken was expected to provide the client with a range of services that included product manufacturing services, such as digitization and imaging services, XML conversion and transformation services, professional services; and editorial services, such as abstracting and indexing. (See Exhibit 1 for project summary.)

The history of the newspaper spanned almost 150 years, from its first issue in 1851 until 1999, which included more than 3.4 million pages and represented a 15-month project for Ken. As per the agreement, Ken had to deliver the first batch (i.e., 10 years of digitized newspaper) within four months of the project's commencement. Thereafter, Ken was to deliver a bulk order of 25 years' worth of digitized newspaper content every two months.

THE PREPARATION: TECHNOLOGY AND CONTENT STRATEGY

Shekhar Sharma, who had recently joined Ken's Hyderabad office, was appointed as project manager for the Genesis Digitization Project. Sharma, an Indian, had six years of experience working for an Indian information technology (IT) company and four years of formal education in technology.

The digitization of *The Genesis Times* represented the first time that Ken had handled a project of this kind. So far, the company had been using the traditional method of web-page delivery, wherein PCs were used to access HTML web pages that were displayed page by page. However, owing to the large volume of data in the newspapers and the requirements of the client, the Genesis Digitization Project could not be carried out using this method. Further, XML was rapidly replacing HTML as a standard format within the industry, and the project required the newspaper data to be converted to the XML format, which demanded an XML-based repository structure. However, compared to HTML and other conventional data sets, the use of XML posed a unique set of challenges. The XML format required creation of rich metadata with a high degree of precision and consistency, as well as a technology-intensive manufacturing environment.

Ken's recently established XML content factory in Tacloban City, Philippines, was thought to be the appropriate location to carry out a large-scale project like this. The factory was equipped with all the tools required to meet the challenges posed by the newspaper digitization process.

A new process and methodology were created for the project. The process involved gathering data from the microfilms, normalizing disparate data formats, digitizing non-digital assets and creating XML files, which were uploaded to the client's digital warehouse. However, to implement the conversion process, it was essential for Ken to operate on advanced technological platforms, which had to be built to facilitate the needs of the project. Such technology development functions were, by and large, performed at the company's office in Hyderabad, India.

Both tasks — content processing and technology development — were indispensable for the project. Keeping this fact in mind, Sharma decided to split the activities of the production and technology development between the Philippines office and the Indian office. It was the first time that the company had adopted this kind of an arrangement to execute a project. The Indian team was given the responsibility of developing a technological platform and transferring it to the Filipino team, whereas the latter was given the task of content processing and production, using the newly developed technical platform.

DISTANT TEAMS, DIFFERENT BACKGROUNDS

Sharma, the project manager, took charge of the Genesis Digitization Project, relocated to the Philippines, and decided to start work simultaneously at both locations to save time. The project started on April 1, 2004.

To carry out the project, Ken created a team of 1,600 employees, with 1,400 members in the Philippines and 200 in India. The Filipino team was segregated into five departments: Production Planning and Control (PPC), Initial Process Imaging (IPI), Document Control and Distribution (DCD), Non-Production Staff (NPS) and Quality Assurance (QA) (see Exhibit 2). The employees in each department were assigned clear tasks. A department manager was associated with each department and was accountable for the department they managed. The Indian team had three assistant managers supervising the project in India in three shifts. Each of the three managers was responsible for delivery from their respective teams.

The Indian team initiated the project through the planning and design of the technological platform, transferring each technology segment to the Filipino team throughout each stage of the development process. While the Indian team was working on the first segment of the technology, the Production Planning and Control department of the Filipino team had the task of receiving the input from the client in the form of microfilms.

The Filipino team members were very comfortable working with the current form of *pragmatic workflow* (a term used for work that required minimal use of high-end technology) since it offered enough flexibility to carry out operations. The members of the Filipino team, however, did not see the benefits of switching over to the new workflow. They were quite sceptical about the new technology that was being developed by the Indian team, and they had reservations about the value of the technology, both to their own team and to the project. Although the team members discussed this issue among themselves, they did not share their concerns with their project manager.

THE WIDENING GAP

While the Filipino team continued to express concerns among themselves about the new workflow, the Indian team was ready with the first segment of the technological platform. The Filipino team received the technology, and its IPI department initiated the scanning of microfilms to create electronic images. The members of the IPI department found the technology frustrating because, in their opinion, it was not very user-friendly and required significant improvement. Michael Tajale, the IPI department manager, complained to Sharma about the issue, and Sharma passed along the feedback about the glitches to the Indian team. The team in India reviewed the feedback and made the necessary modifications in the first segment of the technology and then transferred the revised version back to the Filipino team.

The Indian team then began to work on the second segment of the platform, soon delivering it to the Filipino team. The second segment was crucial for the Document Control and Distribution (DCD) department, which required this platform in order to print the image files to serve as source documents for production.

The DCD department received the second part of the technological platform and got to work. During implementation, however, the employees determined that the technology was flawed, asserting that the glitches in the technology prevented them from continuing their work. The manager of the DCD department, Albert Lumapas, was frustrated with the situation because production in his department had come to a standstill. Further, this unpleasant development increased the Filipino team's concerns about the technology and the team in India, as the team members became convinced that their initial apprehensions had been justified.

HITTING A ROADBLOCK

As the project manager, Sharma, found himself in a quandary because he had never anticipated a situation like this. He realized that he needed to get more involved to straighten out the situation and get the job back on track. With this goal in mind, he convened a meeting with all five department managers and a few employees from each department.

He started off with a general discussion and then gradually began to make inquiries about the delay in the project. He addressed the managers but was met with a stony silence; none of them expressed their concerns. This did not deter Sharma. He insisted that each employee share their views regarding the problems. An employee from the DCC department murmured something about there being a lot of errors in the technology delivered to them and that the team in India was not sensitive to the production department's needs. Sharma took note of the response, tried to find out more about the problem, and asked the employee to explain what the glitches were; however, the employee refused to share anything more. Sharma tried yet again to get answers from the employees, but none were forthcoming. Feeling irritated and frustrated, Sharma lost his temper and yelled at the employees but still could not get a response. He called the meeting to a close.

THE MYSTERY DEEPENS

After the meeting, Sharma urged the Indian team to do their job more conscientiously and also directed them to resolve the errors they had made in the second segment of the technological platform before resending it to the Filipino team.

By this time, it was already May 2004, and things were not improving. Sharma felt genuinely worried about the project. While walking around the production facility, he overheard a conversation in the hallway between Tajale and Lumapas, who respectively headed the IPI and DCC departments.

Tajale: Hey, Lumapas. How's the production going in your department? Are things getting any better?

Lumapas: Not really. There are a lot of issues in the technical part. I don't know what the Indian team is up to. I think they are just not concerned about our problems.

Tajale: I agree with you. While we were working on the microfilm conversion, we had minimal support from the engineering department.

Lumapas: Very true. The other day I sent a very important e-mail to the team in India for resolving a technical issue. It was an urgent one, but there was no answer from the Indian team. Those guys just do not understand the urgency and take their own sweet time to get back to us. My department had to sit idle for the whole day because of the unresolved problem. My team felt frustrated. This was, of course, not the first time that such an incident happened. It's an everyday scenario now with the engineering team.

Tajale: Yeah. That's sad. We didn't have a great experience working with them either. The technology that was transferred to us was not at all user-friendly, and moreover, I feel those guys aren't even looking out for inputs from the production department.

Lumapas: That's right, and this is a big barrier. Our team members are not well versed in the use of technology. Of course, the engineering team didn't organize any knowledge-sharing sessions or training.

The lack of awareness on the use of technology has made it even more difficult for us to reduce the problems.

Tajale: The Indian team did resolve some issues by making some modifications in the technology and transferred that to us a second time. It became all the more complicated to work on those platforms as the rework processes were not clearly defined.

Lumapas: Oh, I see. I wasn't aware of these intricacies. Thanks, Tajale, for sharing this piece of information.

Tajale: Lumapas, there's one thing that I fail to understand. The problem lies with the Indian team, and the project manager keeps asking us, "What's the problem?"

Lumapas: I know, and finally, if something goes wrong, it is always our team that is blamed. Nobody blames them.

Tajale: Yeah … alright then, Lumapas. I have someone waiting for me at reception. I'll catch you later.

Lumapas: Sure, Tajale. Thanks.

After Sharma overheard the conversation, he felt even more perplexed and overwhelmed by the whole situation, which seemed to be rapidly spinning out of control.

THE OTHER SIDE

Sharma believed it was essential to talk to the Indian managers before taking any further steps. Consequently, he connected with Rajeev Anand, one of the three assistant managers in India. Sharma expressed his disappointment over the results delivered by the Indian team. He also asked Anand to clarify why things were not proceeding according to the original plan, to which Anand replied:

> The team here in India has its expertise in developing technology, but at the moment, we are dealing with a new project. This project is not like any of the usual projects and requires a different kind of treatment. Technology of this kind has not been established in the company and thus has required extra time, effort and even refinement. There are a few inevitable bottlenecks in technology at the moment. Despite this, the team is trying to fix all the issues and enhance the applications as and when reported.

> As far as the Filipino team is concerned, sir, I try to ensure that all their concerns are immediately addressed, and they get a timely response. They are not at all patient, and they create an uproar over every petty issue. I believe there aren't as many errors in the technology as they have made out, and I feel lack the inclination to learn the processes involved. I wonder if they even understand the project they are working on. We will, of course, take your suggestions into consideration and ensure successful delivery of the technology.

THE DEADLINE APPROACHES

The project manager's attempts at mediation brought some success. After fixing the errors, the Indian team passed on the technology to the Filipino team, and production in the Philippines finally resumed.

The DCC department printed the image files to serve as documents for production and, thereafter, batched source documents per page for easier data tracking and processing.

Meanwhile, the Indian team was preparing its third segment of the technical platform. As a part of the third segment of technical work, the Indian team engineered links that would enable the Filipino team to provide the abstracting, indexing and other editorial services to the client. This time, they were certain that there were minimal errors.

With the help of the third segment of technology, the NPS department of the Filipino team inserted tags within the content to provide markers that the computer could process. They were also expected to provide the client with certain other services, such as content enhancement, hyper-linking, indexing, abstracting and general editorial services, which once again proved to be taxing for the Filipinos.

The NPS department faced major difficulties in delivering these services. The team members were not able to comprehend the style of language used in the newspaper as they had never been exposed to such writing before. It was with great difficulty that the project moved to the next step.

The IPI department edited the images in this stage. They cropped the corresponding image file according to the pre-coded source document. The project was subsequently passed on to the Quality Assurance (QA) department to perform the procedures required in order to certify that the processed zones met the zoning quality requirement. The department ascertained that the product being extended to the client was of suitable quality and that it met all the required standards. According to the QA department, there were no errors in the digitization of the newspapers.

Despite the team's best efforts, Ken was prepared to deliver only two years' worth of digitized newspapers on July 31, 2004.

THE ANGRY CLIENT

After four months, it was time for the first delivery to be made, as per the agreement. But to the shock of the client, Ken could deliver just two years of digitized newspapers, not even one-quarter of what it had promised.

Not surprisingly, the client was appalled. Dogma International was extremely unhappy, not just with the delay, but also the quality of the delivery. The company issued an ultimatum to Ken: either Ken would deliver high-quality digitized archives of the newspaper, as per the agreement, within a period of two months, or it would lose the project.

The client's warning was a major wake-up call for Ken. The company managers realized that if they wanted to retain the project, they had no other choice but to deliver the product as per the client's requirement. The loss of an important client and potential damage to Ken's own reputation was at stake. The board of the company got together to find a way out. They zeroed in on COO Saiyumn Savarker as their point man to handle the project at this critical juncture.

Prior to attaining this COO position, Savarker had served as assistant vice-president of project delivery at Ken. He had a long and successful record of managing many national and international project deliveries for the company, and the board appreciated his work and the corporate contributions he had made. Savarker flew from India to the Philippines to assess the issue.

THE MISSING LINK

Savarker's primary focus was to get acquainted with the situation. He met with Sharma, who briefed him about the state of affairs and shared everything that had happened during the four-month period. With the information he gleaned, Savarker gained some insight into the client's disappointment with the deadlines, but he still could not identify the source of the problem.

Savarker's next step was to go to the QA department in search of further insights. To his surprise, he was told that the product that had been offered to the client was of good quality. The department manager said, "The team captured the client's relevant content and converted it into XML as per the standards. The 99.95 per cent character accuracy requirement for header information for headlines, sub-headlines, bylines, photo captions, and first full paragraph of the article was ensured. The team also ensured 100 per cent tag accuracy and 100 per cent accuracy for quality pre-audit of the product submitted."

Upon discovering this information, Savarker wondered about the all-important missing link. He decided it would be helpful to find out more from the client, so he promptly arranged for a meeting in order to gain a clear understanding as to why Dogma International considered the product to be inadequate. The client replied by saying, "Though the text part was digitized in a correct manner, the quality of the images was really poor." The client told Savarker that they considered the image part important because it had tremendous power to attract users to the product. With the growth of the Internet, they expected the demand for images to be huge. As the meeting was about to come to an end, the client exclaimed, "At least you talked to us! This is the first time that somebody from your company has asked for input or feedback from us, so we thought our specifications and expectations must be clear to your company."

Savarker returned to his office and met with Sharma. He explained his conversation with the staff at Dogma International and asked Sharma for an explanation. Sharma said, "We weren't aware that the client was concerned about the aesthetics as well. We had no clue about this requirement. If we replace our current scanners with high-resolution scanners, we will be able to deliver high-quality images to the client as per their requirement."

After winding up his meeting with Sharma, Savarker walked directly into his office on the fourth floor. He called his assistant and asked her not to let anybody disturb him for next two hours. He then sat on his chair and said to himself, "There is no time for crying over spilt milk and blaming anybody, but it is sad that this lack of competency or comprehension of the client's need was attributed to poor knowledge on the company's part."

He pondered the situation and realized that Ken needed to digitize approximately 35 years' worth of newspaper afresh, and it also needed to improve the image quality throughout the process. The task seemed enormous since it had to be done within a period of just two months. As he grappled with the situation, Savarker worked towards finding a solution that would steer the project out of dangerous waters.

EXHIBIT 1: PROJECT SUMMARY

Project Description	A newspaper digitization project required to create digital archives of 150 years of the newspaper, *The Genesis Times*.
Input Materials	Newspapers in 35 mm roll microfilm. Each shipment will contain multiple reels. ▪ Each reel may contain several complete issues; an issue will not span more than one reel. ▪ Each issue may contain several pages. ▪ Each page contains a number of articles.
Output Requirements	Both full page and clipped images (of individual article zones) are required. Text will be delivered in XML. For each article (which may include ads and other non-article kinds of individual content): ▪ One XML file, containing all the metadata and zone content for the article. ▪ One tagged image file (TIFF) containing article images. ▪ Exception: photographic zones and charts are to be provided as jpeg images instead of TIFF.
Accuracy Requirement	▪ 99.95 per cent character accuracy for header information (headlines, sub-headlines, bylines, photo captions, and first full paragraph of the article) ▪ 100 per cent accuracy for quality pre-audit of the product submitted. ▪ 100 per cent tag accuracy.
Mode of Transmission	Processed files shall be burn-in DLT tapes

Special Project Requirements	Processed file should be delivered issue by issue directory as follows:
	
	newspaper_issuedate (directory)
	   → each article XML file and all article TIFF
	     or JPEG files from that issue
	   → page (directory)
	     → all full-page TIFF files from that issue
	Each file (whether XML, TIFF or JPEG) will be uniquely named.
	In addition to the required deliverable are:
	▪ exact count of pages in each reel delivered to IDI;
	▪ exact count of pages in each batch delivered to client;
	▪ exact count of articles (by headline) of each batch delivered to the client (transmitted);
	▪ exact count of articles (per batch delivered) not processed.

Source: Company files.

EXHIBIT 2: PROCESS FLOW

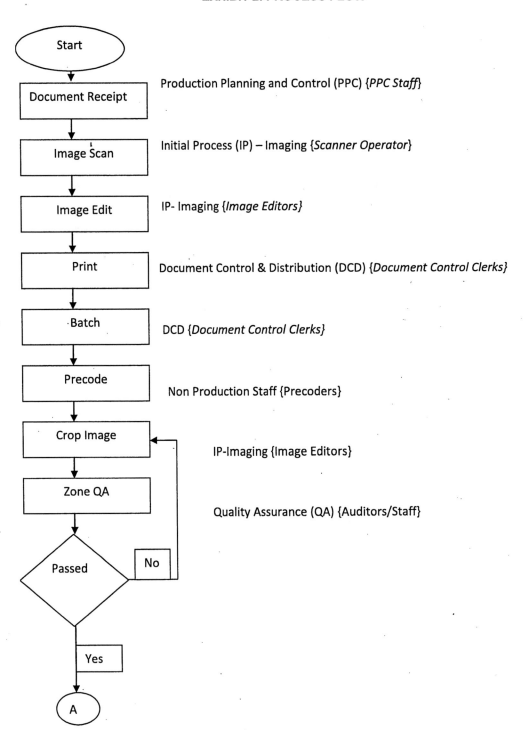

Source: Company files.

Richard Ivey School of Business

The University of Western Ontario

9B05D014

MULTIPLE SCLEROSIS SOCIETY OF CANADA – LONDON-GRAND BEND BICYCLE TOUR

Thomas Kwan-Ho Yeung prepared this case under the supervision of Professor Carol Prahinski solely to provide material for class discussion. The authors do not intend to illustrate either effective or ineffective handling of a managerial situation. The authors may have disguised certain names and other identifying information to protect confidentiality.

Version: (B) 2009-09-28

During the morning of Wednesday, June 23, 2004, Lori Anne McNulty, senior manager of the Multiple Sclerosis Society of Canada (MS Society), Ontario Division, London Office, received a panicked call from Sarah Mann, the supervisor of fundraising events. A major fundraising event, the MS bicycle tour between London and Grand Bend, Ontario, was scheduled for July 24 and 25. Mann was completing a final drive of the route, four weeks before the event when she realized that the road construction would not be completed in time for the event. With the route-planning activities usually requiring 59 days to complete, McNulty wondered whether they would be able to find a safe, paved route and complete the planning activities before the scheduled event.

MS SOCIETY

Multiple Sclerosis (MS) was one of the most common and unpredictable diseases of the central nervous system, affecting an estimated 2.5 million people throughout the world. MS is a progressive disease with symptoms that include loss of balance, impaired speech, extreme fatigue, double vision and even paralysis. Patients' symptoms could be alleviated with medical treatment. People with MS were most often diagnosed between the ages of 20 and 40. In Canada, there were 50,000 people with MS.

The non-profit Multiple Sclerosis Society of Canada (MS Society) provided a wide range of educational programs, client services and medical research support for Canadians with MS. The MS Society also worked in partnership with its counterparts in 39 countries throughout the world.

As a large non-profit organization in Canada, the MS Society comprised seven divisions: British Columbia Division, Alberta Division, Saskatchewan Division, Manitoba Division, Ontario Division, Quebec Division and Atlantic Division. Each division managed and executed its own fundraising activities. Within the Ontario division, 44 chapter offices allowed the organization to reach the local communities. Furthermore, the division offices received guidance and support from the national office.

The Ontario division served 13,000 people with MS, which accounted for approximately 26 per cent of people with MS in Canada. As the largest division in the MS Society, the Ontario division encompassed two fundraising branches: the Toronto office and the London office.

As a senior manager in the London office of the Ontario Division, McNulty assumed the responsibility for all of the aspects of the London office, including the fundraising activities to support the MS research and client services in London. She managed a team of six people and worked in collaboration with the chapter offices.

LONDON-GRAND BEND BICYCLE TOUR

McNulty's main fundraising event was the London-Grand Bend Bicycle Tour. Participants bicycled for two days between London and Grand Bend, located on Lake Huron. On the first day, participants started that day's approximately 85 kilometers of cycling at the beaches of Lake Huron, and made their way toward an evening of entertainment at The University of Western Ontario in London. The next morning, the bicyclists continued their remaining 65 kilometers, returning to Grand Bend for a barbecue, massage, volleyball and swimming. During the ride, the MS Society provided the cyclists with refreshments and services, including emergency support. Each participant was obligated to raise a minimum of $200 from sponsors.

The board of the Ontario Division had established a set of strategic objectives for each fundraising event. For the Grand Bend Bicycle Tour, the goals included $260,000 in donations, an expense rate of 45 per cent, a positive and safe participant experience, and an increased awareness of the MS Society. Considering the strategic objectives and the significant increase in the number of the registered participants, as compared to the prior year, McNulty knew that the route-planning activity was critical to the success of this event. She needed to ascertain that the project met its schedule and that the final route ensured the safety and satisfaction of the cyclists.

ROUTE-PLANNING TASKS AND THE SCHEDULE

In late April, after cleaning her desk of tasks associated with the MS Walk fundraising event, McNulty began working on the subsequent fundraising event, the MS bicycle tour. Working back from July 24, the first day of the event, McNulty established a route-planning schedule in which various tasks and their completion times were specified (see Exhibit 1). McNulty assigned Sarah Mann with the responsibility of completing the tasks identified in this schedule. Meanwhile, the rest of the team focused on food and non-food sponsorship and event marketing for the bicycle tour.

On Monday, May 3, after the threat of snow and the MS Walk event had passed, Mann drove from London to Grand Bend to investigate the two tentative routes: one for each day of the event. The tentative routes appeared to be feasible; for example, none of the bridges was washed out. Mann then called the road departments and county councils to identify whether there would be any planned construction affecting the two tentative routes. After learning that there would be several road construction sites on the tentative routes during the event, Mann revised the routes and drove the new routes to investigate their feasibility for the bicycle tour. Then, she contacted the road department and county councils to determine whether any construction was planned for the revised routes. She eventually learned that there would be a construction site along one of the revised routes, but the construction was scheduled to be completed prior to the bicycle tour. Considering the possibility that the construction would progress on schedule, McNulty and Mann decided to choose this tentative route for the bicycle tour.

The amount of time Mann expected to spend with the roads department and county councils varied considerably due to the high uncertainty involved in finalizing the tentative routes. Once the road hazards were mitigated along the selected route, Mann continued with her route-planning activities by applying for a permit from each of the county councils along the route, which could take four to seven business days. Occasionally, the county councils required a certificate of insurance. Mann typically spent about one day to gather the requests for the certificates before sending the requests to the national office in Toronto.

After obtaining the permits from the county councils, Mann contacted each of the regional emergency service providers for their emergency support: two hospitals, two ambulance providers, six police stations and four fire stations. Mann expected this task to take anywhere from five to eight business days; it was often difficult to reach the correct people from the police and fire stations.

Mann then set the checkpoints for cyclists' rest breaks and estimated the kilometer markings for the route descriptions. There would be 10 checkpoints along the 150 kilometer route. By looking at the route map (see Exhibit 2) and the route description (see Exhibit 3), the cyclists would know the number of kilometers they had completed and the number of kilometers to the next checkpoint. Mann would meet the residents and shop owners along the route to obtain authorization to use their land and/or facilities as checkpoint locations during the event. Due to the difficulty in reaching some people, Mann took about eight to 15 business days to complete this task. Once the checkpoint locations were established, Mann would determine the kilometer description, which took her about one day.

While determining the kilometer descriptions, Mann verified the road conditions along the routes and created a list of locations associated with the emergency phone numbers. It was critical to improve the emergency preparedness of the staff for the event, especially when in rural locations, the emergency phone numbers might not be 911. The phone numbers could be found in blue writing at periodic intervals along the routes. Back at her office, Mann would draw detailed maps, including the checkpoint locations, and prepare both a route description (see Exhibit 3) and a list of locations associated with the emergency phone numbers.

In early July, Mann was scheduled to present the routes to the planning committee of the Grand Bend-London Bicycle Tour and to the staff from Voyageur, an ambulance service provider that volunteered to drive along the route during the event to offer support to stranded or injured cyclists. Then, Mann would print a copy of maps, route schedules and emergency phone number list for the internal users, such as volunteer staff and bike shop mechanics. Mann also made a copy, excluding the lists of emergency numbers, for the external users, such as the cyclists. The external copies were to be distributed to the cyclists on the morning of July 24.

In total, Mann typically required 59 business days to complete all the route-planning tasks. As of June 23, however, only 23 business days remained until the start of the bicycle tour. McNulty commented:

> With Sarah's phone call about the road conditions, we are really in a bind. We were told that the road construction would be finished by now, but clearly that isn't correct. Based on the current road conditions, we don't see how they would be able to finish the road maintenance by July 24. So, we've got to start the planning process on the route all over again. This is incredible. It is just crazy.

With our current registration at an all-time high with 549 cyclists, compared to about 450 registered cyclists at this time in 2003, there is no feasible way to postpone the event. We've already gotten firm commitments from the university, food service providers and many volunteers for those dates. And since the MS bicycle tour is our top fundraiser, I won't even think about the potential of cancelling the event.

Sometimes to complete the tasks on time, we use overtime. I'd prefer not to rely on overtime, if possible, since it can really decrease the staff morale. As it is, the staff will be working the entire weekend, day and night, along with other long days and nights as we prepare for the event. If I can minimize overtime, that could help. Since the MS Society is heavily service focused, staff morale is critical in the interactions with cyclists, clients and volunteers.

We will need to complete the route planning process in a condensed planning horizon. I need to determine our options on how to make this event a success with everyone involved, which includes a safe, hazard-free route.

Exhibit 1

ROUTE-PLANNING ACTIVITIES NEEDED FOR LONDON-GRAND BEND BICYCLE TOUR IN 2004

Activity Tasks	Task Name	Predecessors	Expected Task Duration (Working Days)		
			Optimistic	Most Likely	Pessimistic
A	Drive the tentative routes		0.8	2	3
B	Ask the roads departments for information about the tentative route	A	9	20	40
C	Ask the county councils for information about the tentative route	A	9	15	20
D	Approach county councils for permits	B, C	1	1	2
E	Send requests for the insurance certificate to the Toronto national office	D	0	1	1
F	Obtain the permits from the county councils	E	4	5	7
G	Contact all emergency services	F	5	7	8
H	Set the checkpoints and estimate the kilometer markings	G	8	11	15
I	Determine kilometer descriptions	H	1	1	2
J	Create list of locations associated with emergency phone numbers	H	0.8	1	2
K	Verify road conditions	H	0.7	1	1
L	Draw detailed maps with checkpoints and prepare route description	I, K	1.5	2	2.5
M	Prepare list of locations associated with emergency phone numbers	J, L	0.4	0.5	1
N	Present the routes to the committee and Voyageur staff	L	0.1	0.1	0.1
O	Print internal copy of map and route descriptions	N	0.5	0.5	1
P	Print list of locations associated with emergency phone numbers	M	0.1	0.1	0.1
Q	Distribute internal maps, route description and emergency phone numbers to staff and volunteers	O, P	1	1	2
R	Print maps and route description for cyclists	Q	0.5	0.5	1
S	Distribute maps and route description to cyclists	R	2	5	5

Exhibit 2

THE ROUTE MAP FOR THE LONDON-GRAND BEND BICYCLE TOUR 2003 (DAY ONE)

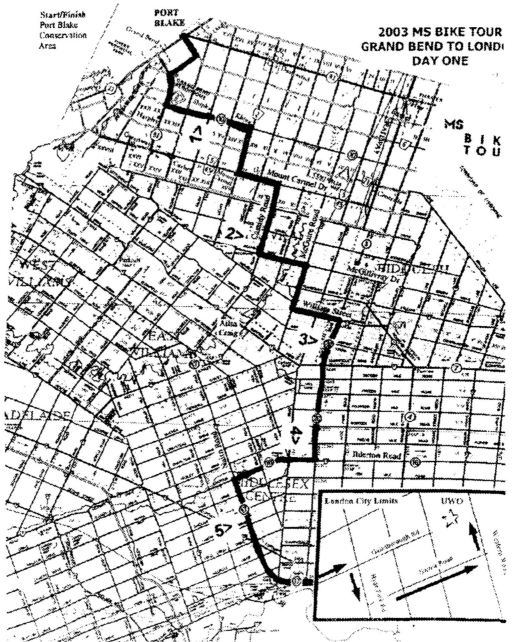

Exhibit 3

THE ROUTE DESCRIPTION FOR THE LONDON-GRAND BEND BICYCLE TOUR IN 2003 (DAY ONE)

2003 GRAND BEND TO LONDON MS BIKE TOUR
DAY 1 (July 26th, 2003)

Route Description

SIGNAL	Exit Port Blake Conservation Area	POINT KM	TOTAL KM
Left	On Highway 21	.2	.2
Right	On Gore Road	3.1	3.3
Right	On B Line	3.1	6.4
Left	On Highway 83	2.8	9.2
Left	On County Road 10 (towards Shipka)	4	13.2
	CHECKPOINT #1		
	Continue on County Road 10	4.3	17.5
Right	On County Road 2 – Bronson Line	4.1	21.6
Left	On Highway 5 – Mount Carmel Drive	4	25.6
Right	On County Road 21, Cassidy Road	5.5	31.1
	CHECKPOINT #2		
	Continue on County Road 21, Cassidy Road	0.8	31.9
Left	On County Road 34 – McGillivray Drive	4.1	36.0
Right	On Maguire Road *Note: Several patches of packed gravel*	4	40.0
Left	On Prince William Street	4.1	44.1
Right	On County Road 20 – Denfield Road	1	45.1
	CHECKPOINT #3		
	Continue on County Road 20	11.7	56.8
Right	On County Road 16 – Ilderton Road	0.1	56.9
	CHECKPOINT #4-LUNCH		
	Continue on County Road 16 – Ilderton Road	6.8	63.8
Left	On County Road 17 (Nairn Rd becomes Gainsborough)	4.3	68.2
	CHECKPOINT #5		
	Continue on Gainsborough	9.2	77.4
Right	On Hyde Park Road	1.2	78.6
Left	On Sarnia Road	5.5	84.1
Left	On Western Road	1	1
Left	Turn onto Wellington Drive (Saugeen Maitland Residence)	0.2	85.3
DAY ONE FINISHED!	TOTAL DISTANCE TRAVELLED		85.3

* km markings are approximate

9A95D015

H.M.S. PINAFORE

                    Version: (A) 2010-02-16

On September 5, 1993, Francis Vanden Hoven, producer of the University of Western Ontario's (Western) Gilbert and Sullivan (G&S) Society, met with his assistant Deborah Carraro, the costume coordinator, Mona Bryden, and the artistic director, Elizabeth Van Doorne, to obtain their advice on how to plan for the performances of *H.M.S. Pinafore* which would take place from Thursday, January 13 to Saturday, January 22, 1994.

BACKGROUND

The University Students' Council (USC), the student governing body which represented Western's undergraduate students and funded projects from school fees, funded the G&S Society. The Society's mandate was to give students, faculty, alumni, and the greater community an opportunity to participate in and enjoy high quality theatre productions at affordable prices. Each year the G&S Society staged a single production.

From 1871 to 1889, during the Victorian age, the well-known English humorist and playwright William S. Gilbert teamed up with the English composer Arthur Sullivan to prepare witty operettas satirizing British society. The quality of both the lyrics and the music made these plays perennial favourites. Each year, Western's G&S Society staged one of the 13 famous operettas on the Western campus in London, Ontario. The 1993/1994 season marked the Society's 40th year.

Francis and Deb had already made a number of key decisions: they had decided to stage *H.M.S. Pinafore*, one of the most popular of the operettas; they had set the ticket prices at $14 for adults, with a $2 reduction for students and seniors; they had decided to have a cast of 40; they had hired a musical director; and, in common with past practice, they planned to stage 10 evening and matinee performances in the 360-seat Talbot Theatre.

The Society operated under a budget set and administered by the USC. In 1992/1993 the total budget had been $28,000 and Francis believed that the 1993/1994 budget would have to be about the same. Although the Society hired some paid staff, particularly musicians, it relied extensively on volunteers in all areas of the production. Although most of the people involved were Western students, about 40 per cent of the cast and crew came from elsewhere in the community. Because the fixed costs such as honoraria, theatre shop fees, costumes, and radio and television advertisements totalled over $14,000, the producer had to be careful managing the variable operating costs.

THE PRODUCER'S JOB

The producer's job was to help the production staff to complete their assigned duties on time. Specifically, his or her duties included:

- along with the production's business manager, formulating a realistic budget to ensure that each department received its financial compensation and behaved in a financially responsible manner;
- assembling primary production and artistic staff;
- booking sufficient suitable rehearsal space for each audition and rehearsal;
- arranging for the rental or purchase of the words (scripts) and music (musical scores) — a different one for each instrument) for the operetta;
- arranging for the sale of tickets;
- in conjunction with the production's advertising director, formulating and carrying out an advertising campaign;
- along with the show's production manager, gathering the secondary production staff and ensuring that they are informed of their duties and obligations; and,
- making a final report to the USC's theatre commissioner.

Thus, the producer had overall responsibility for all aspects of the show. The USC expected him or her to plan the show's major phases, delegate authority to several managers, provide moral support, and ensure that revenues and expenses met budgeted targets. The USC believed that the producer could achieve these ends by being available to all cast and crew, by holding regularly scheduled meetings of department heads and theatre staff, and by keeping the USC informed of all important production matters. Because there were no formal organization chart or lines of authority, control and reporting were more challenging, and open communication was critical throughout the pre-production, production, and post-production stages of the show.

The producer and his or her assistant were typically students who took the job for a single season. Francis Vanden Hoven was in his final year of Western's well-known, two-year honours business administration program. Although he had experience in theatre and was seeking a theatre career, this was his first experience as a producer.

THE MEETING

Francis knew that he would face some pressing issues in the near future. In order to become more familiar with what he was getting into, he invited Deb, Mona and Liz to help him plan for the upcoming weeks. They had had experience with similar roles in earlier years. Francis began the meeting:

Francis: Thanks everyone for meeting on a Sunday afternoon — and on a long weekend too. Deb, I know that you were part of the production last year. Can you give us any advice on how to run things this year?

Deb: Yes, there is plenty that you can learn from last year; we faced some major problems in a couple of areas that you'll have to think about. One was in getting the program completed — was that a headache! Before you do anything else, make sure you hire a publicity director! We can't run any ads without one. They are always tough to come by and it might take you two weeks to find a capable one. After that, you should start working early on the program. You have to get photographs taken of the cast and the crews, and collect biographies of everyone so they can be included in the program. It may take you four to five weeks to get them. Everyone keeps putting it off. After you've collected the information, you will have to enter it into a computer program. That will take a full day.

Francis: What about getting it printed?

Deb: Well that's not so bad. Once you've keyed in all the information, all you have to do is to deliver it on a diskette to the printer so she can complete it. It will take her about five days. This job might well cost you $3,500 after all the adjustments are made, so you want to make sure it is right before you go ahead. It all has to be ready by opening night. By the way, how is your budget coming?

Francis: It is almost done. What a job! I am going to present it to the USC for approval on Tuesday morning. Until they approve it, we can't do a thing. Don't we need the cast arranged before we work on the program?

Deb: Yes, of course we do! We have to nail down the names of everyone in the cast, crew and orchestra before the bios and pictures.

Liz: Of course all that stuff is important, Francis, but don't forget that what really carries this Society is what happens on stage! Now listen. What I am concerned about is getting our set designed and built. That will take six weeks and must be completed before the costume parade — that's when the cast members put on their costumes for the first time. Of course, you will have to hire the production crew before you begin designing or building. Some of them will do a lot of the construction. It might take four weeks to find them. Who really knows though? That is the price you pay when you rely on volunteers. We also need to train the production crew for their stage work. That might take 12 days. We should advertise in the student paper to attract volunteers. We could kill three birds with one stone by using the same ads for the publicity crew, the production crew and the cast. I think you can get advertising space for about $40 right now and it will probably take a week. You've hired a set designer, right Francis?

Francis: Well, not exactly....

Liz: You haven't! All you producers seem to worry about is the bottom line. You have to have a set designer before you can design and build the set or train the stage crew. You should spend some time selecting your set designer, because a well designed set is critical for a high quality show. This shouldn't take you any longer than two weeks. We will also have to arrange to audition and choose the cast. We should be able to get through them in a couple of days — probably a Friday and Saturday — but we will have to advertise first and make sure we arrange a time and a place with a piano. We should try Talbot Theatre again but they may be busy so allow a week to get a place. What about the music, Francis?

Francis: Well, we have hired Chuck Baxter as musical director. He has had quite a bit of experience with G&S productions in the past, both as musical director and also in other roles. Once the USC approves the budget, he will recruit the orchestra members and arrange to get the sheet music. It will probably take him a week to recruit and a week to get the music.

Liz: Look, we have to have music before the cast starts rehearsals. I would like to rehearse on a regular basis for three hours each Sunday afternoon and Monday and Tuesday evenings every week for 12 weeks. Don't forget about the Christmas exam and holiday period. Exams start on December 5, and run through to about the 22nd. The exact duration varies from student to student but when you have a cast of 40 you can essentially write off the whole period. Students are understandably reluctant to do much either during or just before exams. We also have some trouble in late October when many write mid-terms and essays. And, the university will be officially closed from December 23 to January 3. Even if our cast and crew is in London, we won't be able to get access to Talbot Theatre to practise or build the set during that time. And, that is just days before opening night. Will Chuck get the scores on time?

Francis: Let me check and get back to you. The orchestra will only rehearse for about four days though, so they won't need the music immediately.

Mona: Francis, Liz's sets and the cast are important but don't forget about my costumes! That's when my job begins. I will need some basic supplies and someone to help me out. After I collect the supplies and measure the cast, we can go ahead and order costumes from Toronto. The whole thing should take about a week, even allowing for delivery. However, just to be sure, I would like to have them here a week before we absolutely need them in case there are any problems. The total cost shouldn't exceed $6,500. Sometimes I can negotiate an extra 10 per cent discount.

Francis: What happens once the costumes arrive?

Mona: Then I will have to organize a costume parade to ensure that there are no problems before opening night. Invariably, some costumes will need to be altered. The costume parade and alterations will take about five days but shouldn't cost much — but it works best if the set is complete first so we can get a better idea of how the costumes are going to work. Right after the costume parade we can do our dress rehearsal. That is the first time when it all comes together. We only have one dress rehearsal a day or maybe two before opening night. That is the first time that the orchestra and the cast actually work together. And, of course, the stage crew works that one too.

Deb: Oh yeah, and one last thing Francis. Don't forget about publicity — you wouldn't want to forget about selling tickets, would you? Once you've hired a publicity director, you can advertise and then select a crew to develop an advertising plan. It will take about four weeks in total. It shouldn't take more than about a week to develop a plan, but after that we should blitz all types of advertising media over about three weeks. It is important to take the time to hire capable crews — after all, they are volunteers and if they do a poor job, the whole production, and all of us, will suffer. It might take you up to four weeks or so, but it is probably worth it. Don't forget that your time is valuable too, though!

Francis: I am sure we have lots of time. But, if something goes wrong, can we speed up any of these activities if we have to? And, by how much? And, how much will it cost?

Deb: Well, Francis, we can probably speed up most of the things we have to do. You have to be careful though. Don't forget that we are dealing with volunteers here. They are committed but we don't pay them anything and they do have other responsibilities. If you push them too hard they might quit and there isn't much you can do about it. If that happens, especially at crucial times, we are toast.

Liz: Yeah, that's right Deb. But, there are some things we can do, especially on the activities we pay for. For example, if we spent more on advertising, we could attract more good candidates and shorten the time to find the crews by a couple of weeks. And, we could also get the printer to speed up by doing it on overtime. I think we might be able to get it done in only two days if we were prepared to spend an extra $750.

Mona: And, that costume place will do the same thing for an extra $100 per day. We could get them delivered in 48 hours if we paid for it. With our small budget, though, I wonder if it is wise to spend our money that way.

Francis: What about the set? It is one of our primary activities.

Deb: Well, we obviously couldn't get the time down to zero. But, by hiring an extra master builder we could probably knock a week off. Don't we pay about $80 per day for the master builder now?

Francis: Yes, that is what last year's budget was. What about rehearsals? Can we speed them up?

Liz: We could, but again we have to be careful. The orchestra isn't much of a problem. But, if we push the cast for more hours per week we will run into problems with cast members not having time to absorb the material and with rehearsals interfering with their other activities. We might lose some of them. And, if we cut down on the total time, we won't look as polished as I would like come opening night.

CONCLUSION

Francis summed up his feelings:

> We want to have the most professional looking production we can for our money. We have certain standards we would like to keep, such as the glossy posters and radio and television ads.

> But the true test will come in the music, singing, dancing and acting on opening night. A great opening night performance will generate the newspaper reviews and the word of mouth that will either make or break the run of the show. All the producer can do is set the stage and attempt to have everything flow in an organized fashion.

> After I get the budget approved on Tuesday, I will need a schedule so that I can prioritize my time. Although many tasks can be performed at the same time, I have to know which ones are critical so I can focus on them. After all, I am a full-time student in a tough program and I can only be a part-time producer. Right now I am only concentrating on

what needs to be done up to opening night. I will worry about the clean-up activities later. I will also need a more complete budget so I can make some of the tough financial decisions.

Exhibit 1

CALENDAR FROM AUGUST 1993 TO JANUARY 1994

August

Sun	Mon	Tue	Wed	Thu	Fri	Sat
1	2	3	4	5	6	7
8	9	10	11	12	13	14
15	16	17	18	19	20	21
22	23	24	25	26	27	28
29	30	31				

November

Sun	Mon	Tue	Wed	Thu	Fri	Sat
	1	2	3	4	5	6
7	8	9	10	11	12	13
14	15	16	17	18	19	20
21	22	23	24	25	26	27
28	29	30				

September

Sun	Mon	Tue	Wed	Thu	Fri	Sat
			1	2	3	4
5	6	7	8	9	10	11
12	13	14	15	16	17	18
19	20	21	22	23	24	25
26	27	28	29	30		

December

Sun	Mon	Tue	Wed	Thu	Fri	Sat
			1	2	3	4
5	6	7	8	9	10	11
12	13	14	15	16	17	18
19	20	21	22	23	24	25
26	27	28	29	30	31	

October

Sun	Mon	Tue	Wed	Thu	Fri	Sat
					1	2
3	4	5	6	7	8	9
10	11	12	13	14	15	16
17	18	19	20	21	22	23
24	25	26	27	28	29	30
31						

January

Sun	Mon	Tue	Wed	Thu	Fri	Sat
						1
2	3	4	5	6	7	8
9	10	11	12	13	14	15
16	17	18	19	20	21	22
23	24	25	26	27	28	29
30	31					

Designates a statutory holiday in Ontario.

THE TORONTO SUN AND CARIBANA

INTRODUCTION

As another work day quickly came to an end, Samantha Morrison finished up a few emails, returned a missed phone call and sat down to prepare for the following afternoon's meeting with her boss, Larissa Presso. She knew she would be in the office late that night, trying to make sense of the barely started, unorganized project that had recently been thrown onto her lap for rescue.

Presso, the director of promotion for the Toronto Sun, a daily newspaper publication in Toronto, Ontario, Canada, notified Morrison a few days earlier of her new project. The Toronto Sun was a major media sponsor for the world-famous Toronto Caribbean celebration, the Scotiabank Caribana Festival. It was Morrison's responsibility to organize the newspaper's involvement in the major parade, which was an important part of the festival.

It was June 5, 2008, and Morrison was beginning to feel the pressure. The project was originally assigned to Morrison's colleague, who failed to make any real progress. It was Presso's decision to ask Morrison to intervene and take over. Morrison knew it would be a lot of work to assess the current progress and determine the next steps.

She questioned whether it was feasible to be finished by the date of the parade, on August 2, at 10:00 a.m. It was imperative that the Toronto Sun had a float, because it had already paid for its sponsorship and all of the other major sponsors would have floats in the parade. Morrison wanted to do a great job because it was an interesting project for her and because she wanted to impress her new employer.

SCOTIABANK CARIBANA FESTIVAL

Scotiabank Caribana Festival was a two-week cultural celebration of Caribbean music, cuisine and visual and performing arts. The title sponsor was Scotiabank, a major Canadian banking institution. Approximately 30 other companies also sponsored the festival as major or minor sponsors; the Toronto Sun was one of the major media sponsors. This Toronto-based festival began in 1967 when the Canadian government approached the Caribbean community to request its involvement in celebrating the country's centennial year. Organized by a group of 10 individuals living in Toronto, the festival set a standard for the years to follow. Its goal was to develop a platform to showcase the beauty, joy and music of Caribbean culture.

Scotiabank Caribana Festival had been celebrated in Toronto every year since its inception, had become a major international event and was the largest cultural festival of its kind in North America. The two-week event culminated with a large parade featuring dancers, costumes, musicians and extravagant floats. Parade weekend was usually the first weekend in August, which coincided with Simcoe Day, the day marking the abolishment of slavery in Upper Canada in 1810.[1] Scotiabank Caribana Festival had become an expression of Toronto's multicultural and multiracial society. It was an important event, which attracted people from around the world.

SAMANTHA MORRISON

Morrison had recently been hired as senior promotions coordinator at the Toronto Sun and her job demanded exceptional task management skills, as she was always working on several projects at one time. She joined the company with extensive experience in events co-ordination, marketing and public relations. A graduate of Ryerson University in Toronto, Canada, Morrison earned a Bachelor of Applied Arts in Radio and Television Broadcasting. While concentrating her studies on television, she also minored in English. Some of her courses included public relations, performance, business, media writing, television theory and broadcasting.

Morrison had a lot of experience in the media industry. At a young age, she worked hard to ensure that she immersed herself in as many opportunities as possible. In high school, Morrison completed a co-op placement at a local television station, working with the production crew and often on screen as a reporter. In addition to the task of on-air host for featured news and events, Morrison worked in the graphics department and in the studio as the floor director. Passionate about extending her knowledge beyond what could be offered in the classroom, Morrison remained very busy throughout her university career volunteering and working for a variety of big name companies in the entertainment and media industry. Morrison worked in the promotions department of two significant Toronto-based companies: Inventa and Bensimon Byrne-Dynamo Living Media. With this initial experience in promotions and event co-ordination, Morrison was able to land the job of street team coordinator for Alliance Films. Upon graduation, Morrison sought a full-time position with Alliance. Although the company was not offering at the time, Morrison received a referral from a colleague for a job with Arcade Agency, a marketing and creative firm. As an account coordinator, she earned experience in generating status reports and coordinating communications between clients and account managers.

At the age of twenty-four, only six months after her graduation, Morrison received an offer from the Toronto Sun to work in the promotions department. The position required strong skills in coordinating and managing various events throughout the year, acting as an ambassador for the company and promoting a strong public image for the firm.

---

[1] *In 1810, Upper Canada was defined geographically as the area presently known as Southern Ontario. Upper Canada was established in 1791 when the British Parliament passed the Constitutional Act, dividing the province of Quebec into two distinct areas along the present-day Quebec-Ontario boundary — Lower Canada in the east, and Upper Canada in the west.*

THE TORONTO SUN

The Toronto Sun was a paid-circulation daily newspaper distributed throughout Southern Ontario, Canada. A division of Sun Media (Toronto) Corporation, the newspaper was born out of The Toronto Telegram Newspaper on November 1, 1971. After two successful years, in 1973 the publication expanded its Monday-through-Friday print to include the Sunday Sun. In September of 1986, the newspaper expanded once again, offering the Saturday Sun, making it a seven-day publication.

Sun Media Corporation was a wholly owned subsidiary of Quebecor Media Company (TSX: QBR.A, QBR.B). The company was Canada's largest newspaper publisher, with a mission to "help connect and build better communities" across the nation. Sun Media had forty-three paid-circulation and free dailies in Canada's key urban markets, as well as two-hundred community publications. Printing news for both the English and French communities of Canada, the publisher captured 10.5 million readers each week.

THE TORONTO SUN CARIBANA PARADE PROJECT

With eight weeks left until parade day, Morrison recognized the urgency of a meeting with Presso to propose her plan for the project. While Morrison and Presso had spoken briefly about the project when it was assigned to Morrison a few days prior, Morrison wanted to run her detailed plans past her boss before proceeding further. It was already Thursday and she had set up a meeting with Presso on Friday at 1:00 p.m. Preparing for the next day's meeting required a lot of work. Morrison planned to do some research on previous Caribana Parades, the logistics and the Toronto Sun's prior involvement. As well, she wanted to be sure she understood the history behind the festival. She knew it would also be useful to research information on the company's recent involvement with any other parades. She could start her research at the Sun Media News Research Centre immediately. The Centre was inaccessible after 7:00 p.m.; therefore, Morrison had only two hours to get the information she needed. Information from the Research Centre and the Internet were the only sources Morrison would reference. Previous co-ordinators no longer worked with the company; however, Morrison believed that Presso's experience would be helpful throughout the process.

At the meeting, she knew that Presso would provide her with the contact information for their go-to person on the festival management committee (FMC), the team responsible for co-ordinating the various facets of the Caribana Festival. Morrison planned to call their contact and review the details of the parade day and float requirements to confirm her discussions with Presso. If she could get hold of them before the end of the day Friday, she expected the conversation to take less than an hour. However, chances of reaching them in their office so late on a Friday afternoon were slim, and thus Morrison might not be able to move forward with the planning until Monday or Tuesday. Worst case, it could take up to a week to reach someone, since it had been months since Morrison's colleague last spoke with anyone on the team.

Since her meeting with Presso was not scheduled until 1:00 p.m. on Friday, Morrison had time Thursday evening and Friday morning to prepare a timeline and task schedule. She would need as much time as she could get.

Designing the Float

As Presso had explained in their previous conversation, upon speaking with the FMC representative, the design stage of the float could begin. Morrison would be ready to meet with the Toronto Sun design department at that stage. Before the meeting, reviewing previous floats and brainstorming ideas would be critical. In previous years, the Toronto Sun float had been very simple with a few representatives riding the float; Morrison hoped that she could make the float more creative. The difficulty was working with a minimal budget. Presso had indicated that the project would receive a $400 cash budget to be used toward paying the driver of the float. Morrison needed to obtain all other materials and services by means of contra advertisements,[2] valuing the space at the transient or open-line rate. (Exhibit 1 provides the transient rate along with some of the other 2008 advertising rates.) This also meant that her sources for materials and services would be limited to those companies and individuals with whom the Toronto Sun already had an existing account; the time crunch left no time for establishing new advertising partners. Morrison believed her meeting with the design department could be scheduled for about one day after talking with the FMC representative.

In the meantime, Morrison also needed to hire a contractor to build the float. She saw no reason why the preliminary stages of the hiring process could not be started at the same time as the design stage. The first thing she would have to do was define selection criteria for the Toronto Sun's contractor needs (about four hours). Next, Morrison would need to obtain a list of approved vendors from the advertising department. After receiving the names and contact information (approximately four hours), and after the meeting with the design department, she could call the various contractors to obtain information on their services (about three hours), rate them according to her selection criteria and choose a contractor (no more than two hours). After selecting the contractor, Morrison could proceed to rent a flatbed truck and hire a driver for parade day — it would take about half a day to choose the truck and driver and finalize the arrangements. The driver would be required for at least eight hours on parade day to guide the float on the parade route. She could hire the driver on a contract basis for $26/hour.

After meeting with the design department, Morrison expected to receive a draft design within three to five days. She would have to review and return the draft with her feedback and comments as soon as possible; this would take her about a day. The design department would then return the final design to her in about a day. Then, if Morrison was pleased with the department's revision, she could move on to obtaining approval for the design. Otherwise, the design re-drafting could take up to four rounds back and forth between her and the design department, lasting as long as one week. Once satisfied with the float design, Morrison would need to forward the plans to Presso for approval. But since Presso was exceptionally busy with out-of-office meetings and conferences that month, it would take at least five days for her to review and approve the draft. When the final draft was approved, it could be forwarded to the float contractor so that they could begin building. The contractor would be responsible for all building materials, while Morrison would need to obtain any decorations or aesthetic elements on her own.

The float construction would happen in two phases. The first phase could be completed before parade day. Once the contractor received the approved design draft from Morrison, they could purchase the materials required for building (half a day). Then they could prepare the major pieces of the float by cutting the wood to the required dimensions and assembling sections of the float. If they worked efficiently, this task would require two days to complete. The second phase would be completed on parade day morning, when the flatbed truck arrived at the parade site. The contractor would then assemble the float and finish construction.

---

[2] *"Contra advertisement" is a term used for the means of advertising that is paid for with goods or services, and not money.*

Volunteer Management

Morrison believed that while the decorative design elements depended partially on available vendors, the one element of the Toronto Sun's presence in the parade that she could guarantee was the volunteers. The people riding the float would be an important part of the day. Morrison planned to have volunteers dressed in brightly coloured "Toronto Sun Caribana" t-shirts. The volunteers would need to be energetic to draw the crowd's attention. In addition, the volunteers would toss giveaways into the parade crowds, including necklaces made in the fashion of Mardi Gras, assorted candies and whistles. Following her meeting with the design department, Morrison planned to send an office-wide email inviting staff, and their family and friends to participate on the float. Over the next three weeks, she would receive RSVPs and could also address any questions or concerns the volunteers might have. She hoped to get at least forty-five volunteers. Once she confirmed a final count on the number of volunteers, Morrison could develop ideas for parade day volunteer kits. Each volunteer would receive a bag containing a parade day t-shirt, snack foods such as granola bars and fruit, sample size sunscreen and water bottles. To obtain each item, Morrison planned to approach some of the newspaper's advertising partners. She figured this would take about three days.

The t-shirts for parade day would need to be designed by the design department. Morrison would send a request to the team outlining her needs. Within eight to twelve business days, she should receive design ideas from the design team. To aid in the selection process, Morrison would need to consult Presso, as well as the vice-president of advertising, Mark Print. Their review and design selection would take no more than four days. Immediately after receiving the RSVPs from the volunteers, Morrison could obtain preferred t-shirt sizes from the volunteers, which would probably take two to three days by the time everyone responded to her. This way, she would be able to forward her order for the t-shirts to the production firm, Custom Press, as soon as the design approval came in. T-shirt printing should not take more than seven business days. Using regular shipping services, the shirts would be shipped and received within two to three days following printing. With an additional fee of $25, the process could be expedited and Morrison could guarantee the shipment within one day.

The final phase of the volunteer management pre-parade involved the volunteer safety waiver forms. In the initial meeting for this project, Presso had explained to Morrison:

> In order to incorporate volunteers on our float on parade day, we must ensure to follow legal procedures strictly. You will need to contact our human resources (HR) department to request the appropriate volunteer waiver forms. In the past, HR has responded to requests within two days, usually requesting the full names of all volunteers. After receiving the list of volunteers, HR can prepare the forms and forward them to the legal department for review (approximately one day). Since the legal department always seems to be overworked, you should count on a significant delay in its response. Often, it has taken up to two weeks to complete the requested forms. HR will then send the forms to you — since they are hard copy, they go through inter-office mail (usually takes one day). Once you receive the waiver forms, you will need to mail them to the volunteers with a postage-paid return envelope. You need my approval to charge the mailing fees to our department, but I should be able to get it to you within the day that you are ready to mail. Expect, however, to receive undeliverable and returned mail. Be prepared to obtain any final signatures on unsigned forms on the day of the event as the volunteers arrive. It is important that all participants sign a waiver form.

Entertainment and Other Materials

As Morrison continued to reflect on the planning involved in participating in the parade, she suddenly realized that she had overlooked one of the most important elements of the float: entertainment! Following the final approval of the float design, Morrison knew she could begin the process of hiring entertainment. The Caribbean celebration was rich in cultural music and Morrison needed to brainstorm ideas and scope out potential talent. She could do this step within three to seven days. She realized there were three options: a live band, a live radio DJ, or pre-recorded music. After contacting potential entertainers (two to four weeks), Morrison would discuss her top choices with Presso. The meeting would take only two hours, but Presso would likely need one to two days before being able to meet. After selecting the entertainer, she would confirm their availability for parade day and have them sign the contract (half a day).

Also following final approval of the float design, Morrison could work on obtaining the crowd giveaways. It would probably take her a few weeks, but it could be done in parallel with other tasks. Finally, Morrison needed to request advertising banners from the marketing department to dress the outside of the float. Requesting and receiving the banners would take from seven to 10 days.

All of these tasks, including the flatbed rental, hiring the driver, prepping major pieces used in float assembly, receiving the banners from marketing and t-shirts from Custom Press, mailing the waiver forms, obtaining parade day giveaways and hiring the entertainer, needed to be completed by Friday, August 1, at 5 p.m. After that time, all the vendors and the internal Toronto Sun departments would be closed for the weekend and thus Morrison needed to have everything in place before then.

Parade Day Tasks

Morrison's work as project manager would not be complete until the Toronto Sun float reached the end of the parade route. On parade day, Morrison would have many tasks. The first thing she would need to co-ordinate was the final assembly and construction of the float. Once the driver and flatbed truck arrived at the parade start, the contractor could finish the float. When the contractor finished his work, which should take no more than two hours, Morrison could decorate the float with the advertising banners and other aesthetic elements. Within three quarters of an hour, Morrison would need to check in with the FMC. After signing the float in, Morrison would need to meet with all the volunteers, obtain any outstanding signatures on the safety waiver forms and distribute the volunteer kits. Next, the giveaways would need to be secured on the float and split into several containers so that volunteers at each end and side of the float would have easy access to them while on the parade route. In addition, Morrison would need to store all of the volunteers' carry-on items in a safe place on the parade float. Finally, along the parade route, it would be Morrison's primary responsibility to manage the volunteers, entertainment and truck driver. She expected to work about eight hours that day.

As Morrison reflected on the daunting task ahead of her, the extent of the workload suddenly began to sink in. She glanced over at the clock and realized that forty-five minutes had already passed. She needed to get over to the Research Centre to begin her research as soon as possible. Before her meeting with Presso, she knew that she would need to date the project tasks to determine if the float would be completed by the parade day, August 2. If not, she needed to either figure out a way to get it completed on time, or pull the float from the parade — although then the Toronto Sun would lose the valuable marketing exposure that it was entitled to as the primary print media sponsor.

Exhibit 1

THE TORONTO SUN ADVERTISING: PARTIAL RATE CARD — EFFECTIVE JANUARY 2008

DISPLAY RATES
ANNUAL LINAGE CONTRACTS
PER AGATE LINE

	MON.-SAT.	SUN.
TRANSIENT	$7.06	$ 10.24
3,000	$6.64	$ 9.62
5,000	$6.50	$ 9.42
10,000	$6.35	$ 9.21
20,000	$6.14	$ 8.90
30,000	$6.00	$ 8.70
50,000	$5.72	$ 8.30
75,000	$5.58	$ 8.09
100,000	$5.37	$ 7.78
150,000	$5.23	$ 7.57

COLOUR ADVERTISING RATES

PER AD	MON.- SAT	SUN.
B/W plus 1 colour	$4,156	$4,780
B/W plus 2 colours	$4,695	$5,398
B/W plus 3 colours	$5,552	$8,070

Note: 1,600 lines constitute a full-page advertisement.
Source: Company records.

Richard Ivey School of Business

The University of Western Ontario

9A98D020

PROCTER & GAMBLE CANADA: DAYQUIL SAMPLING OPERATIONS

Version: (A) 2010-01-27

INTRODUCTION

Looking over his shoulder, Ken Mark noticed that once more, he had a new voice message. The "new message" light had been blinking constantly for the past few hours, and this was starting to cause him concern. "It's probably Lance again," he muttered. "Wish I could promise him that our DayQuil samples will be ready for the October 6 shipping date, but I can't. At least not yet. At this rate, we might not be able to get them till *next* year, and it seems as if there's nothing I can do about it."

It was August 1, 1997, and on the eighth floor of the Procter & Gamble building in Toronto, Mark, a summer intern from a top Canadian business school was evaluating his few remaining options. How did this logistics nightmare arise? Could he still save the DayQuil sampling program or would it have to be scrapped for this year? He was sure he had the solution in front of him, somewhere within the dozen or so messages. Had he missed any key details?

The DayQuil topper sampling project first involved getting Canadian artwork and copy for the cardboard shell and the DayQuil foil pouch. Alongside this timeline, Ken had to co-ordinate processes to ensure that the samples were packaged and shipped on time. Ken had a hunch that he was way behind schedule. But how far behind was he?

Lance Wade, the national category manager for Procter & Gamble's OTC (over the counter) medication had bumped into Ken in the hallway just after 12 noon. "You're going to have the DayQuil toppers for my October 6 start of ship, right? I know you can do it," Lance said, "We're counting on you." The urgency of the situation finally hit home and Ken realized that he had to get his act together.

With 5 p.m. fast approaching, he knew he had just a few hours left to figure it all out. He shook his head: Why did he leave this to the eleventh hour? Krista Boone, the Quils brand manager would be at his cubicle in half an hour, and Mark was certain he needed to craft a solution before she arrived. Being new to project management, it all seemed like absolute chaos to him. It was like trying to hold on to sand slipping through cupped hands. At this point, every extra day mattered.

PROCTER & GAMBLE (P&G)

Based in Cincinnati, Ohio, Procter & Gamble had operations in more than 70 countries. Its Canadian division was part of the North American region and was based in Toronto, Canada. It employed over 800 people in the main office building, and had numerous production plants scattered throughout the country.

Since they introduced Ivory Soap in 1879 — one of the world's first advertised brands — P&G has been on the leading edge of marketing innovation. They have pioneered many of the approaches that have become marketing fundamentals in every part of the world, from advertising and product sampling to concepts like brand and category management (see Exhibit 1). Most important, they continue to strive for marketing leadership in every part of the world where their brands are sold.[1]

P&G's brands were split into four divisions; Laundry and Cleaning products, Paper products, Health Care & Beauty Care products, and Food & Beverage products. NyQuil and DayQuil belonged to the Health & Beauty Care division, which, in 1996, had $1.4 billion in sales and included other brands such as Scope, Crest and Formula 44.

KEN MARK

Hired as an assistant brand manager for the summer, Ken was looking forward to working at P&G, long known as the premier marketing company in the industry. After two years in the Faculty of Kinesiology at The University of Western Ontario, Ken had accepted a place in the Honours Business Administration (HBA) program at the Richard Ivey School of Business at UWO in the fall of 1996.

Ken had a very high need for achievement and his past record bore that out. As a high school student, Ken had organized several conferences for student leaders, often taking entire weeks off school for these endeavors. Although he ended up missing a considerable amount of class time, Ken was always able to keep up with class assignments and graduated from high school with a 91 per cent average. In addition to his interest in student leadership issues, Ken was also a serious athlete, having taken up the triathlon as his sport of choice. Despite not knowing how to swim when he started, Ken saw this as simply one more challenge. With this interest in sport and the competition that it fostered, Ken began his university education in kinesiology, taking such diverse courses as modern dance, accounting, biomechanics, and business French.

During his first year in the HBA program, Ken earned a reputation as a strong individual. In addition to his shoulder-length hair, his willingness to take often controversial positions in class marked him as someone unafraid to stand alone and defend his viewpoints. Normal, cautious approaches rarely appealed to him. But, he was no troublemaker; the business school setting reinforced the need to respect authority and to work in a team-based setting.

---

[1] *From their Website "www.pg.com"*

THE QUILS BRANDS

Richardson-Vick's NyQuil and DayQuil were introduced to the Canadian market in the 1960s, and were not selling as strongly as their U.S. counterparts. Around June 1997, NyQuil and DayQuil combined to represent just under three per cent or 2.5 million units of the Canadian respiratory market.

The large and often confusing variety of medication available to consumers meant that as a category, the cold remedy section was difficult to shop. (Exhibit 2 shows a typical layout of a pharmacy.) In this fragmented category, all brands needed to show growth and hit a critical mass to maintain listings. It was not uncommon for small brands, with insufficient growth, to be delisted from a national retail chain. Although currently a small brand, DayQuil clearly had potential.

Ken's summer internship at P&G

In May, during the early weeks of Ken's summer employment, he was given the DayQuil topper sampling project to manage, along with other projects such as the Quils test market and Scope brand analysis.

The most feasible option to grow DayQuil's share in the market (aside from television advertising) was to sample DayQuil caplets on NyQuil bottles, encouraging sales of NyQuil and DayQuil. Contained within P&G's targets were plans to rapidly increase market share of both NyQuil and DayQuil. For perspective, the U.S. DayQuil brand was able to double market share within three years as a result of various promotional projects.

For DayQuil, a brand strategy would be charted to relaunch the brand with a sampling and media drive. This approach would increase new user trial of DayQuil, and encourage current NyQuil users to purchase DayQuil as their daytime medication. Obviously, there was growth to be achieved with DayQuil because as of June 1997, not all NyQuil consumers used DayQuil as their daytime medication.

Ken had initially thought this would be rather simple; "How difficult can it really be?" he exclaimed to Krista. "All I have to do is redesign the graphics and copy on the cardboard topper, and develop bilingual copy for the foil pouch. Print them out, package them and ship 'em out the door! It won't be that tough — once it's done, what will I be doing for the rest of the summer?" Krista just smiled and shook her head knowingly.

The DayQuil Topper Sampling project[2]

To sample DayQuil caplets on NyQuil bottles required that a foil pouch containing one dosage of DayQuil (two caplets) be folded and placed within a cardboard topper (holding the pouch in place.) The topper would then be fitted over a NyQuil bottle, packaged and shipped to the stores. (See Exhibit 3 for an example of a DayQuil topper and foil pouch.) Before these operations could be completed, however, artwork and copy had to be printed on the cardboard topper for consumer appeal and to meet Canadian health regulations. These activities were managed through an artwork packaging process.

The artwork process seemed complicated, but Pat Egan, P&G Health Care's process co-ordinator, who worked with several brands in the Health Care division, explained it thus:

---

[2] *Terms and actual lead-times for the P&G artwork process have been changed to protect confidentiality.*

To create the DayQuil cardboard topper that will hold the DayQuil foil pouch containing a sample of the medication, we usually start with the design brief. A design brief contains all the details and objectives for the artwork. I have allocated seven design phase days for this step. This is written by you and reviewed by our legal department; once approved, we can move to the draft phase.

Design manager Ron Zamorski will review the design brief during a planning meeting and provide feedback to me. If done right, this will only take an hour. Then I will contact Diane Miller from the purchasing department and Kate Marrale from the tech packaging department to secure printing time. Before I do this, however, it is your job, Ken, to get the blueprints of the U.S. topper from U.S. Brand. I'm not going to do that for you. It took the previous project person four days to transfer the file.

In the interim, I can set up a process to send the digital blueprint to Design Partners, our design studio, and submit claims for legal opinion. Because of the other projects I am working on, this should take me one day. But this process can happen while you are transferring the file. Alexandra LeClair, who works for Design Partners, is currently assigned to your project and will send you a preliminary copy of the designed cardboard topper for your inspection once she receives the U.S. blueprints; it usually takes her one day to do so. The draft ready step, which is the end of the draft phase, involves Ron Zamorski's sign-off on the project. This does not take any time, provided that there are no glitches along the way. He usually does not have any major concerns, and although it has taken up to three days (due to the fact that he might be away on business), Ron is V usually very prompt with sign-offs (about one day).

Ken looked at the timeline he had sketched out and realized that he was already past the design brief phase and into the draft phase. From further conversations, he had discovered that because this sampling project involved medication, it required an extra step before Ron signed off on the document. Thomas Deng, from P&G's regulatory department, reviewed all OTC (over the counter) packaging that would be seen by the consumer, to ensure that there would be no problems with Canadian regulations. This step would take an extra three days at least, as he had to review the standards set out by Canadian health authorities.

Krista had walked over to Ken's cubicle and remarked,

Hey, we might just be able to borrow 120,000[3] units of ready-made foil pouches from the U.S.; their brand manager was very accommodating and said he'd do his best to help us out. It could take from two to four weeks to get permission, but it looks feasible. There are concerns, though, that I would like you to look into. I've got to put out other fires at this time, but I will be dropping by later to see how you're progressing.

But before I go, I should update you on some things. By now you've heard that we will have to oversticker the foil pouch with Canadian artwork (which, for all intents and purposes, was a duplicate of the artwork and copy on the DayQuil topper cardboard shell.) But you know that the pouches that we are getting have an expiry date of February 1998. Well, the retailer will not accept anything less than six months to the date of expiry, as you know. Good news: we might just be able to extend the date by one

---

[3]*Please note that numbers have been changed to protect confidentiality.*

year, legally, of course.[4] I think that it will take around two weeks to get the papers through our claims department once the U.S. approves, and an okay from regulatory would take another two days.

From previous experience, it took up to two weeks for Canadian customs to clear unusual shipments of medication. I am wondering if this could be sped up if calls are made in advance to customs officials. Before this happens, though, U.S. DayQuil said that it would take four to five days to schedule packing of the foil pouches for shipment.

Once we receive the foil pouches, the Canadian Health Protection Board (HPB) will want to inspect the contents, and it usually takes up to one week for this to happen. Sometimes they take longer if they are tied up with other work.

I have to do two things today: First, finalize with U.S. brand if we need to borrow the 120,000 units, or tell them not to worry about it for this year. Second, tell Lance if he can count on us to have the DayQuil toppers ready by October 6. I'll be back shortly.

Ken knew that if that the project were not ready for October 6, it might as well be canceled, because it would mean that the deadline for shipment to P&G's trade customers would be missed. It all came down to whether the U.S. foil pouches *and* Canadian artwork could arrive at the packaging contractors no later than September 23. Another issue was raised: What if consumers were able to peel off the oversticker on the U.S. foil pouch and were confused by seeing conflicting expiry dates? One way to deal with this issue would be to talk to P&G's quality assurance department and discuss it with upper management. Because this was becoming a priority, discussions with upper management would take a day to arrange. The quality assurance department, however, would require more time to come to a conclusion, as they had to research several outcomes. It would take from five to seven days to perform this step. Of course, the project would still have to be given a risk rating from the legal department before proceeding, and this would take a day or two.

Picking up the telephone, Ken called Pat to inquire about the rest of the steps concerning the artwork for the cardboard topper and the pouch. Pat continued:

The last step, to conclude the draft phase, involves agreement from Ron, which can usually be secured immediately. Then we will prepare and send the initial design files to Design Partners (two to three hours), and the initial Acrobat (a computer publishing software program) file is sent to me from Design Partners (it takes five days), and a copy is forwarded to you for approval. This is the start of the artwork packaging phase. Our legal department usually takes five to seven days to approve the claims made, and the sell copy. If they have any issues, you have to spend an extra day or two to resolve them. I would recommend doing it right the first time, as it can get time consuming. On our side, we will have a preproduction meeting.

For your information, the preproduction meeting involves checking ink draw-downs, prepress testing, and having photos and illustrations finalized. This takes between two to

---

[4] *An extended expiry date for the U.S. DayQuil caplets could be sought. It was perfectly legal and safe according to Canadian health guidelines, which meant that P&G could proceed with this option with no objection from any Canadian health regulatory or legal agency. The biggest concern was a potential for consumer confusion due to differing expiry dates.*

four days. Then Linda Hampshire from my department will identify any graphics issues. She takes less than two days to finish her assignments.

The preproduction meeting and Linda's work can be done while you are getting legal approval. Once these steps are complete, technical copy can be finalized by you (it will take at least one day, trust me) and the technical specifications sheet is then finalized by me within a day. If we are prepared, both these items can be accomplished within the same day.

Next, translation of approved copy into French as per Canadian regulations will take you guys at least three days. Remember that this is only the first round of Acrobat, and there can be up to three rounds if any of us are not fully satisfied. Then, the final Acrobat file is approved by all of us and sent to Design Partners. This should take five days. Once they receive it, it will take another five days for them to process and return the final Acrobat file to us.

Also, there are always changes to be made, and words have to be translated once again with the final Acrobat file. This will take up to two days. Because this is also the final file, both our legal department and upper management will have to approve it. Both will take five days each to do it, but they can be done in parallel. One more thing: management approval is contingent on Ron signing the design frozen document once Canadian brand (that's you) finishes the artwork packaging approval document. It takes at least four days for you to get signatures for artwork packaging approval documents. That concludes the artwork packaging.

Are you confused yet? (Ken nodded his head.) Well, here is the last step: printing tools. Once Alexandra gets approval to proceed, she can send the files to the print house where thermals are made, along with the separations. Cylinders are also engraved at this point. Count on 10 to 14 days for this step. Actual printing will take five days, and then the printed cardboard and over-sticker can be sent out to the packaging contractor within a day. Well, that's all for now.

After finishing his discussion with Pat, Ken began thinking about previous conversations with Steve Sherwood (P&G's industrial buying department). Ken knew that the packaging contractor who would oversticker the U.S. foil pouch, fit it in the printed cardboard topper, and place it on the NyQuil bottle, would need seven to nine days for this operation. Although it was only a small amount that was being prepared for shipping, each oversticker had to be hand-applied. Also, cardboard toppers had to be individually folded. This was a very time-consuming process.

Ken looked at his watch. Half an hour had already passed. Trying hard to remember what he had learned in his operations management classes concerning crashing timelines, he sat down to figure it all out. He had wanted this summer internship to be a challenge, something substantial with real issues to grapple with. Whereas there was no long-term impact associated with taking a strong position during classroom case discussions, he knew that if he stumbled with the DayQuil topper project, it could affect other people as well.

His job in the next while would be to figure out if it was possible to make the October 6 deadline. If it were possible, the next step would be to figure out how to make it happen. But, if it did not look as if there would be any choice but to cancel the project, Ken had to have solid reasoning behind his recommendation. Krista wanted to know either way.

The phone rang and it was the contract printer on the line; "Mr. Mark, in order to be certain that the oversticker arrives in time for September 23, we have to order it today," said John Howard. Ken knew that it would mean committing to a $25,000 cost. "And we also have to book time on the printing schedule now," John continued. "Would you like us to proceed?"

Exhibit 1

CURRENT BRANDS AT PROCTER & GAMBLE

Exhibit 2

THE PHARMACEUTICAL SECTION IN A TYPICAL STORE LAYOUT

Exhibit 3

EXAMPLE OF DAYQUIL TOPPERS AND NYQUIL BOTTLES

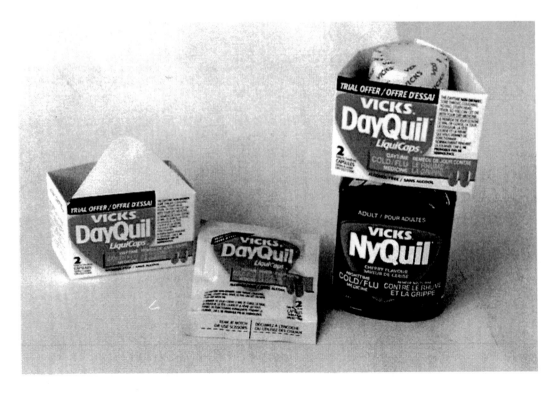

A07-14-0001

KAREN A. BROWN
NANCY LEA HYER
NATHAN T. WASHBURN

GLOBALMED: TELEMEDICINE
FOR THE RIO OLYMPICS

The 2016 Olympic Games were fast approaching and Manoel Coelho, Director of Global Business Development at GlobalMed, knew this left him with very little time to accomplish his goal: taking telemedicine technology and services to the Rio de Janeiro Olympic Games in Brazil, his home country. Telemedicine offered opportunities for delivering high-quality data sharing, diagnosis, video consultation, and treatment decisions in real time to patients and clinicians who were separated by physical distance. Coelho recognized that successful application of telemedicine for Olympic athletes and spectators could amplify exposure and accelerate its worldwide adoption. Coelho's more specific near-term goal was to keep GlobalMed, based in Scottsdale, Arizona, USA, in the line of sight as the telemedicine vendor of choice for the Olympics. Exposure during the Games could potentially offer worldwide brand awareness for the company. GlobalMed's longer-term goal was to gain a foothold in the Brazilian market, which offered significant opportunities for telemedicine penetration and a springboard for growth into South America. The following hypothetical scenario, a composite of several real stories, describes how GlobalMed officials envisioned the role telemedicine could play at the Games:

A badminton player representing Japan suffers an eye injury from a fast-moving shuttlecock in one of the early rounds of women's doubles competition during the Rio Olympics. She is pulled from play. Medical personnel located on site conduct preliminary exams using a portable telemedicine station and convey results to a Rio hospital, where ophthalmologists specializing in retinal injuries review photographic and ultrasound images. The player is transported to the Rio hospital, where additional images and diagnostic tests are run. Brazilian specialists make the decision that the eye injury is too serious for the player to continue participating in the Games. This news is communicated somewhat awkwardly through an interpreter. The badminton player is devastated by the ruling—she has trained for 15 years with Olympic competition as a lifetime achievement goal. Understanding her distress and the far-reaching implications of the decision, her family helps her connect with a renowned retinal specialist in Kyoto. He contacts the ophthalmologists in Rio and requests all images and records be conveyed to him via the encrypted, cloud-based telemedicine system. He also conducts a virtual, live exam and speaks with the player using the telemedicine unit's video capabilities. Upon careful review and consultation with his colleagues in Kyoto, he determines that the injury should not exclude her from participation in remaining Olympic matches if she adheres to a short-term treatment regimen, along with the recommendation that she wear protective eyewear. He advises that her eye condition should be monitored carefully before, during, and after each match to ensure that it is stable, and communicates his need to be fully connected via telemedicine for all of these tests. Based on the assessment from Kyoto, the Brazilian ophthalmologists reverse their decision, and the player is allowed to continue competing. A telemedicine unit, fitted with special-purpose cameras, an ophthalmoscope, and an eye ultrasound monitor, is used courtside three times during each match to assess the eye condition, which does prove to be stable. The player continues with her doubles partner through the remainder of the competition, and they finish with a silver medal. This allows her to achieve her life's dream, and also sets her in motion to compete in her home country in the 2020 Tokyo Olympics. The story could have ended very differently without the support of telemedicine, which facilitated a rapid, accurate, and thorough response with real-time input from specialists in the athlete's home country.

Coelho worked closely with Dr. Antonio Carlos Marttos, a fellow Brazilian and world-renowned expert on medical trauma who was based at Jackson Memorial Hospital's Ryder Trauma Center in Miami, FL, USA. Marttos was the chief spokesperson selling the telemedicine concept to Olympic officials. As Marttos envisioned it, the Rio Olympics project would place about 11 portable telemedicine units in competitive event sites, to serve both athletes and spectators, as well as an additional portable unit in the Athletes' Village. Given the critical nature of health to an athlete's performance and career, access to personalized medical care was essential, and sometimes had been a missing link in previous international athletic events. Additionally, the technology would offer major benefits to spectators who might experience medical emergencies while attending events. Exhibit 1 shows a GlobalMed portable telemedicine unit similar to the ones proposed for use in the Rio Olympics.

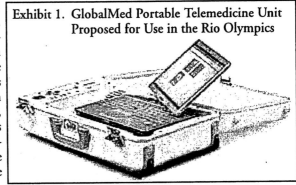

Exhibit 1. GlobalMed Portable Telemedicine Unit Proposed for Use in the Rio Olympics

GlobalMed: History and Performance

GlobalMed was founded in 2002 by Joel E. Barthelemy,[1] whose previous entrepreneurial endeavors were in integrated learning systems and semiconductor quality control. His experiences had enlightened him about the broad potential for using remote cameras to virtually diagnose technology problems in the semiconductor quality process, and he recognized that the concept had applications in the growing telemedicine industry. A camera, on its own, would not be enough to create a robust and comprehensive telemedicine system. Full function would require an integrative software platform to support numerous pieces of diagnostic and communication hardware, a state-of-the-art IT system for capturing and transmitting images and data, high-level data security, and a network of trained medical professionals who would make the entire system work.

Barthelemy funded GlobalMed with his own resources for the first seven years of the company's existence, and later added supplemental funding from six angel investors. By 2014, the company had over 100 employees. It had generated substantial profits,[2] and had been recognized for rapid growth by several entities.[3] For example, Inc. 500 ranked GlobalMed in the top 100 fastest-growing U.S.-based companies, and seventh in healthcare for 2012. *Deloitte's Technology Fast 500*[4] ranked GlobalMed 58th for growth in 2012, up from 122 in 2011. Revenues were $32 million in 2012 and $27.4 million in 2013. This revenue decline, the first in the company's history, was caused primarily by a budget stalemate in the U.S. Congress that delayed until 2014 some major purchases of GlobalMed equipment. New contracts in the U.S., Latin America, and the Middle East indicated that 2014 would be a banner year for sales. Nonetheless, revenue trends made clear the importance of establishing a broader international portfolio of clients.

In 2014, GlobalMed executives recognized that a well-crafted international expansion strategy was needed to sustain positive momentum. Brazil, the market focus for the Rio Olympics project, was one of several key areas for global expansion. According to Detelina Trendafilova, Director of International Business, other high-priority geographic areas included Chile in South America and Romania in Europe. Chile's economic strength and its linear geographic layout made it a logical location for extension beyond Brazil. Romania represented an attractive target because, according to Trendafilova, it already had one of the most advanced telehealth systems in Europe and had committed to wider-scale adoption. This focus on global expansion was consistent with the company's stated mission: "To transform healthcare globally by developing and integrating secure, efficient health delivery systems that improve access and quality of care, while eliminating unnecessary costs."

Organizational Structure

GlobalMed's structure (see Exhibit 2), designed to foster cross-functional interaction, was flat and informal. The company applied a matrix approach in which initiatives ran horizontally through the various functions, and employees were assigned on a temporary and part-time basis to serve the changing needs of GlobalMed's project

2

A07-14-0001

portfolio. The organization was too small and the portfolio too broad to allow for full-time team assignments to individual projects. Brad Schmidt, Director of Strategic Accounts, played a central integrating role in coordinating efforts across departments for major initiatives, such as the Rio Olympics.

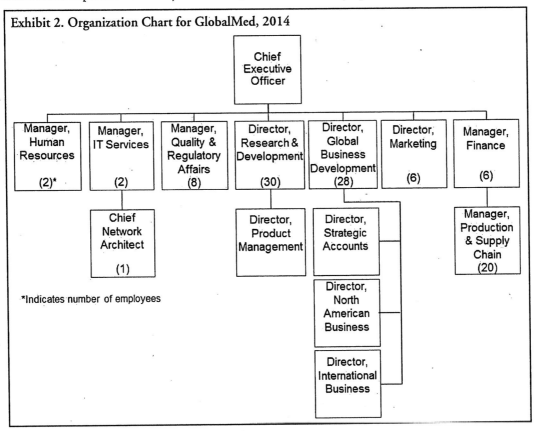

Exhibit 2. Organization Chart for GlobalMed, 2014

GlobalMed's Competitive Differentiators

GlobalMed was one of a multitude of players in the telemedicine industry. No single player was able to provide everything necessary to make a telemedicine unit operable, so collaborative partnerships were prevalent. GlobalMed assembled fully functioning telemedicine stations that combined some of its proprietary equipment and services with equipment and services from other companies. GlobalMed executives believed they had created competitive advantages that were responsible for the company's rapid growth within the industry.

First, according to Coelho and Schmidt, a major differentiator for GlobalMed was its commitment to quality and regulatory compliance. As a matter of policy, GlobalMed worked diligently with regulators during the full development lifecycle of new technologies and product modifications. The company had eight people[5] assigned full time to these areas, which represented a proportionately larger allocation of resources than any of its competitors. The company was an ISO[6] 13485: 2003-registered medical device manufacturer. Additionally, GlobalMed had sought and maintained International Electrotechnical Commission (IEC) 60601 Ref. 3 certification, also from the International Organization for Standardization (ISO), making it one of the few in its industry to possess this global qualifier.

A second competitive strength was GlobalMed's capacity for integration. When fully assembled and activated in the field, a GlobalMed station brought together all functions seamlessly. For example, its secure, cloud-based systems offered the highest level of data and image security while allowing for integration across a wide range of information systems. This was important for the array of organizations that would be connected through a telemedicine network because it eliminated the need for file conversion across platforms. Further, GlobalMed's manufacturing arm had the expertise to customize as needed and assemble all technology into one unit, allowing for turnkey deployment upon delivery to the customer. Also along the lines of integration, company officials felt confident that GlobalMed's eNcounter™ software provided a better, more medically specific interface than any of the more general applications its competitors offered. Yet another aspect of integration was the training and service GlobalMed offered as part of its contractual relationships with companies purchasing its equipment. Training was an area where GlobalMed was expanding its offerings as part of its strategy to ensure closer, long-term relationships with clinical end users.

The DICOM (Digital Imaging and Communication in Medicine) standards adopted across GlobalMed's stations, via its CapSure®[7] and CapSure Cloud®,[8] offered a third competitive differentiator. These technologies allowed fully encrypted images from every GlobalMed telemedicine station to be transmitted with all related patient data embedded in the files.

Distributed Sales Model

GlobalMed had developed strategic alliances with several companies, including HP, Lifesize, Microsoft, Avaya, Cisco, and Polycom. These companies and their channels offered some of the physical components, IT products, and system support necessary for telemedicine units. A significant part of initial sales contacts came through these partner organizations, which then contacted GlobalMed and began working with a member of the GlobalMed sales team to create a proposal. The major players in GlobalMed's partner network often had their own resellers who might actually be the point of contact for customers, so the length of the sales chain could put GlobalMed at a significant distance from end-user customers. By 2013, the company had begun to engage more actively in efforts to create name recognition with institutional end users in the U.S. Moreover, GlobalMed's international expansion strategies were moving toward direct connections with clinical customers, and the company planned to build its global sales force and ongoing revenue streams accordingly.

GlobalMed's Products, Services, and Markets

GlobalMed's telemedicine stations, supported by customized back-end software, facilitated real-time interactions between patients and doctors, allowing patients to be examined through the use of GlobalMed's DICOM-compliant software, exam cameras, stethoscopes, vital signs monitors (including pulse oximeters), spirometers, ophthalmoscopes, otoscopes, ultrasound devices, EKG monitors, and a variety of other devices that could be integrated into telemedicine stations. (Appendix A describes these devices.) Hardware sales represented 85% of GlobalMed's revenues, with the remainder coming from recurring fees for ongoing support and maintenance.

Exhibit 3. Example of a Full-Featured GlobalMed Telemedicine Station

As of January 2014, GlobalMed's installed base of full-featured telemedicine stations totaled over 3,000, and the company had about 300 orders either confirmed or in the pipeline. Approximately 90% of installed stations and future orders were for U.S. locations; however, international sales had tripled in the previous two years. Most international sales were small-scale deployments designed to gain market entry. According to Neal Schoenback, Director, North American Business Development, this mirrored the growth strategy that had worked well in the U.S. market. Beyond its full-featured units, GlobalMed had sold several hundred mobile units and many more of its clinical components, including medical exam attachments and over 10,000 of its general exam cameras for use in telemedicine units sold by other companies. An example of a typical full-featured telemedicine station is shown in Exhibit 3.

GlobalMed's most substantial sales relationship was with the U.S. Veterans Administration (VA), where more than 1,600 of its telemedicine stations were installed in satellite clinics in rural communities and connected to major VA facilities. The telemedicine stations facilitated virtual face-to-face exchanges and remote diagnosis, both for patient-to-clinician and clinician-to-clinician interactions.[9] Based on VA data, the number of telemedicine consultations exceeded 1.4

4

A07-14-0001

million in 2012, and GlobalMed estimated there were over two million consultations in 2013. This was the largest telemedicine deployment in the world, to date, and it had attracted attention and new sales from many international government entities.

Another successful GlobalMed partnership was the Telestroke program that linked stroke specialists at Mayo Clinic Hospital, Phoenix, Arizona, with 13 rural and remote hospitals in Arizona, Missouri, and New Hampshire. The 24/7 service provided rapid assessment, diagnosis, and emergency treatment decision-making, which were critical to long-term outcomes and quality of life for patients with stroke, and the Telestroke program had delivered very positive clinical outcomes.[10]

GlobalMed also had made inroads with the U.S. Corrections System, where a mobile telemedicine station could be taken directly to an inmate's cell, reducing the risks and costs associated with transferring a patient to a clinic inside the facility or to a hospital outside the facility. As of early 2014, the company had sold 41 units to the State of California, 17 to the State of Oregon, and five to the State of Florida.

GlobalMed kept itself on the cutting edge of technical development with a strong R&D team led by Michael Harris. Harris and his team worked continuously to develop new products and refine existing ones. The R&D team collaborated with the Product Management group, led by Ashley Droege. Droege and her team had responsibility for discovering new customer needs through their activities in the field. Miniaturization was a key part of GlobalMed's product development strategy. For example, the company was developing diagnostic hardware and software to work with "MyCapSure™," a new smart phone medical photo-sharing application. The GlobalMed interface would allow encrypted patient data to be transmitted to a clinician, who could then provide feedback to the patient about what he or she should do under certain conditions. Many smart phone applications were appearing in the market, but none could promise the data security GlobalMed would offer. Miniaturization and smart phone applications offered the potential to move telemedicine into the home, reducing the requirement for a patient to travel to a clinic. It also offered potential for expanding the reach of telemedicine in international, multi-venue sporting events such as the Olympics.

The Rio Olympics Project

The 2016 Rio Olympic Games offered a significant opportunity for GlobalMed. With over 10,000 athletes from 244 countries competing in 28 sports across 306 events, the chances for injuries and ailments were significant. Dr. Marttos played the central role in pitching the telemedicine idea to the Brazilian and International Olympic Committees. As Marttos emphasized in a May 2013 speech to the American Telemedicine Association (ATA), if an injured athlete could connect with a specialist in his or her home country, language and cultural barriers would be diminished as obstacles to diagnosis. Moreover, home-country doctors, familiar with the athlete's medical history, career goals, and personality, could offer a more holistic perspective. So, although any country hosting the Olympic Games was likely to have its own trained specialists with the highest ethical standards and best interests of the athletes in mind, connecting with doctors from an individual's home country presented great appeal.

Marttos also emphasized the role telemedicine could play in reducing spectator concerns about the availability of healthcare services in medical emergencies. He argued that the assurance of available care and virtual connections to home-country doctors could increase the number of Olympic visitors. This had become an especially significant issue in light of the 2013 Boston Marathon bombing incident that killed three people and injured nearly 300 others,[11] and the 2013 Russian suicide bombings during the weeks leading up to the 2014 Winter Olympics.[12] Underscoring Marttos' concern about medical care at international sporting events was a January 2014 communication from the U.S. State Department warning spectators planning to attend the Sochi, Russia, Winter Games about potential inadequacies in the region's medical system.[13]

Telemedicine offered the potential to reduce the strain on Rio's 10 major hospitals serving a population of 6,000,000. The city's medical establishment, challenged to meet existing demands,[14] would have difficulty accommodating the increased load created by an influx of the 1,500,000 tourists projected to visit Rio for the Games.[15] But, even if additional medical personnel were imported for the two-week event, there was no guarantee the right specialist would be in the right place at the right time. Telemedicine could deliver expertise on short notice, an important consideration in a city whose transportation system was navigated through numerous water inlets and granite peaks via congested tunnels, bridges, and narrow roadways that created some of the most bottlenecked traffic in the world.

The Rio Olympics were viewed as a jumping-off point for GlobalMed's plans to enter the Brazilian market and gain first-mover advantage in telemedicine there. Brazil, with the world's fifth largest population,[16] fifth largest land mass,[17] and sixth largest gross domestic product,[18] made sense as a strategic target.

GlobalMed's Activities Leading Up to the Rio Olympics Initiative

GlobalMed had worked toward the Rio Olympics project for several years, making progress that would draw it closer to winning the bid as the telemedicine vendor of choice. For example, Coelho closely followed the 2011 Pan American Games when telemedicine, involving video-conferencing only, was implemented there under Dr. Marttos' leadership. It was effectively used several times, including one instance where a gold-medal volleyball player injured her spine in a fall. A team of specialists in Brazil, in collaboration with Dr. Marttos, shared secure image and data files, and made treatment decisions that ultimately allowed her to sustain the viability of her career. For the 2012 London Olympics, Dr. Marttos and the University of Miami selected GlobalMed to provide a portable telemedicine unit to support the Brazilian team. This represented a landmark in Olympic Games history because it was the first time a fully integrated telemedicine unit, complete with medical device attachments, had been used in the Games. The unit proved itself valuable in multiple instances. For example, the ultrasound device on the mobile unit was used ringside in boxing events several times to test for damage following major abdomen blows.

Beyond the international sporting event industry, GlobalMed's pioneering work with offshore oil platforms in Brazil had offered the company a vehicle for gaining Brazilian government approvals for its devices, and for obtaining precedent with import licenses. Telemedicine was a valuable tool on oil platforms; on-site diagnosis of an injured worker could reduce the number of unnecessary helicopter transports, which were both dangerous and expensive. In another Brazilian application, many victims of the January 27, 2013, Santa Maria Night Club fire, that claimed 236 lives and injured over 100 others, were screened and treated on site, 606 miles (975 km) south of São Paulo, with the help of the GlobalMed portable station that had been used during the London Olympics in 2012. The technology facilitated remote assessment of burn damage to inform decisions by physicians at Albert Einstein Hospital in São Paulo about whether and where victims needed to be transported, or how they could be treated on site.[19] These success stories added to GlobalMed's credibility and offered proof of concept for telemedicine with the Brazilian government and with the Brazilian Olympic Committee.

Financial Considerations

GlobalMed had donated its time, equipment, or expertise to support pilot tests of telemedicine in both the 2011 Pan American Games and the 2012 London Olympic Games. However, for future events, the company expected client investments. If the equipment were sold at going rates, about $20,000 to $30,000 apiece, the 12 units, accompanied by annual charges for support services, estimated at about $5,000 per unit after the first year of operation,[20] would produce a relatively small amount of revenue.

Assuming GlobalMed were selected as the telemedicine vendor for the Games, the official ROI for the project was likely to be low or negative. However, potential media exposure could offer great value. GlobalMed could not afford the cost of official Olympic sponsorship, so the company would not be able to mention the Olympics in its advertising and would need to rely on and facilitate exposure in the news media to achieve its brand recognition and market penetration goals.

Scope of Work for the Rio Olympics Telemedicine Project

The Rio Olympics project would involve a complex set of interrelated tasks, many of which would require support from global partners. An important consideration was the Brazilian cultural propensity for last-minute decision-making.[21] GlobalMed officials anticipated the final decisions about whether to adopt telemedicine and which vendors to select would occur within three to six months of the start of the Games. Consequently, an important

A07-14-0001

aspect of GlobalMed's project strategy would involve being ready to deliver as soon as it had an official order. Capacity for quick delivery could be the key factor in the Brazilian Olympic Committee's decision about which company to select as the telemedicine provider.

Coelho and Schmidt, along with the informal cross-functional team they had assembled, spent some time brainstorming a preliminary set of activities for the project, but they acknowledged they might have missed some important elements. They also recognized that some of the items on their list could be considered major deliverables, and others were detailed tasks that might need to be clustered together under a higher-level deliverable category. Examples of activities the team identified for the project included the following:

Activities	Background
Product development	GlobalMed's R&D team needed to ensure that when the time came for a vendor decision, its equipment was the most state-of-the art and simple to use. The equipment's functionality and capacity to meet the needs of a major sporting event would be important deciding factors.
Supply chain	Vendors would need to be selected and orders placed for components not produced by GlobalMed. Some of these components would have lead times exceeding the potentially short lead time the Brazilian Olympic Committee was likely to give the chosen vendor.
Training practitioners: Brazil and athletes' home countries	Telemedicine represented a new application for nearly all of the doctors who would potentially be involved. Part of the training would be technical, but part of it would be aimed at increasing acceptance among practitioners. Dr. Marttos articulated the most important challenge: "You can buy the equipment, but the human network is the most important thing."[1] The Ryder Trauma Center, under the direction of Dr. Marttos, had already begun training teams of nurses and doctors from Rio de Janeiro in intensive two-week telemedicine programs in Miami.[2]
Transportation of devices to Brazil	The units would have to be shipped in a safe, secure, and timely manner and would need to arrive far enough in advance of the Games to allow time for clearing Brazilian Customs, testing, training, and installation.
Repair and maintenance	Repair manuals would have to be available in Portuguese, and Brazilian repair personnel trained for quick response. Additionally, a cache of spare parts would be necessary.
On-site support team for the Games	GlobalMed would need to select, train, and deploy a support team to attend the Games and be on hand to assist with use of the equipment. This would ensure that the GlobalMed units were working to their maximum potential, and would also allow for discovery of media opportunities.

[1] Interview with Dr. Marttos, August 2013.
[2] http://www.jacksonhealth.org/ryder-telemedicine-borders.asp, accessed 22 January 2014.

Opportunities and Challenges Ahead

Coelho had invested his time in multiple trips to Brazil in pursuit of the Olympics telemedicine project.[22] He enjoyed full support from the top—Barthelemy, GlobalMed's CEO, viewed Brazil as the company's top priority for emerging market entry. Additionally, the Olympics project had strong internal support among GlobalMed stakeholders from all key departments, who saw the potential the project offered for expanding the company's market share and increasing brand awareness. They recognized that even if GlobalMed were not selected as the primary vendor for the Games, the company would potentially benefit from the increased exposure for telemedicine.

In spite of the potential upside it offered, the project was complex and vulnerable to risks. The more risks GlobalMed team members could anticipate, the better prepared they would be for dealing with them if they materialized. As previously mentioned, the Brazilian culture was known for indecisiveness and last-minute decision making. Additionally, Brazil's equivalent to the U.S. Food and Drug Administration (FDA), known as ANVISA (Agência Nacional de Vigilância Sanitária), imposed significant regulatory barriers for medical devices. For example, in December 2011, one of GlobalMed's units, which had been used temporarily on an oil platform, was detained in Brazilian Customs for five days before it was allowed to be returned to GlobalMed in the U.S. Another significant risk had to do with adoption by clinicians, who might resist the new technology because it represented a major disruption to traditional healthcare delivery models. There were likely to be many other challenges, and the project team was in the process of tackling a comprehensive risk assessment.

Endnotes

[1] To view video posts from Barthelemy's blog, see http://www.globalmed.com/telehealthanswers/category/take-note-with-joel-barthelemy/, accessed 19 December 2013.

[2] Revenues grew 32-fold from 2007 to 2012, and although most recent years had shown positive growth, it was not as rapid as it had been between 2007 and 2010.

[3] For details, see http://www.globalmed.com/about-globalmed/globalmed-awards.php, accessed 3 November 2013.

[4] The *Deloitte Technology Fast 500* rated the 500 fastest-growing technology companies by region, based on percentage revenue growth over five (EMEA and North America) or three (Asia Pacific) years. See http://www.deloitte.com/view/en_US/us/Industries/technology/technology-fast500/index.htm, accessed 3 November 2013.

[5] Five of these individuals reported to the Quality and Regulatory Affairs Manager and three reported to the Production and Supply Chain Manager.

[6] ISO is the International Organization for Standardization. http://www.iso.org/iso/iso_catalogue/catalogue_tc/catalogue_detail.htm?csnumber=36786, accessed 16 October 2013.

[7] The DICOM-compliant software connected easily to CapSure Cloud® cloud-based services, allowing secure access to medical images by remote clinicians.

[8] Cloud-based DICOM Picture and Archiving and Communication System for Management of Visible and Nonvisible Light Images.

[9] http://ee.usatoday.com/emag/Default.aspx?href=USAM%2F2013%2F11%2F04&pageno=1&view=document, accessed 16 January 2014.

[10] Based on an interview with Bart Demaerschalk, MD, Director of Mayo Clinic's Telestroke Program and Professor of Neurology, Mayo Clinic College of Medicine, 17 December 2013. Also see C. V. Fanale and B. M. Demaerschalk (2012). "Telestroke Network Business Model Strategies," *Journal of Stroke & Cerebrovascular Diseases*, 21(7): 530-534.

[11] http://online.wsj.com/article/APf9eaafde8b424309a52bcbef567fa6e0.html?KEYWORDS=Boston+Marathon. Also see http://online.wsj.com/news/articles/SB10001424127887323308504579087520408939790?KEYWORDS=Boston+Marathon, accessed 27 November 2013.

[12] P. Sonne, "Russia Places Olympics on 'Combat Alert'," *The Wall Street Journal*, January 8, 2014, A8.

[13] D. M. Herszenhorn, "U.S. Cautions Americans Attending Winter Games," *The New York Times*, January 11, 2014, B12.

[14] In 2013, the Brazilian government imported 6,000 doctors from Cuba, Portugal, and Spain in hopes of easing the demand burdens. See http://articles.latimes.com/2013/may/11/world/la-fg-wn-brazil-cuban-doctors-20130510, accessed 19 November 2013.

[15] In massive demonstrations and riots that began in June of 2013, Brazilians voiced their concerns that the government was spending excessively in preparation for the Olympic Games and other sporting events, while ignoring public services and healthcare needs. See http://fusion.net/justice/story/brazilian-spring-explainer-22554 and http://www.economist.com/blogs/americasview/2013/06/protests-brazil?spc=scode&spv=xm&ah=9d7f7ab945510a56fa6d37c30b6f1709, accessed 19 November 2013.

[16] Following India, China, the United States of America, and Indonesia.

[17] After Russia, Canada, the United States of America, and China.

[18] After the United States of America, China, Japan, Germany, and France.

[19] See http://www.globalmed.com/press-room/press-releases/2013/distant-specialists-use-telemedicine-for-survivors-of-brazilian-nightclub-fire.php, and http://finance.yahoo.com/news/distant-specialists-telemedicine-survivors-brazilian-130000097.html, accessed 27 November 2013.

[20] All units were sold with a one-year warranty on the technology, and extended packages were available.

[21] See S. Branco (2005). *Brazil: A Quick Guide to Customs and Etiquette*. Portland, OR: Graphic Arts Center Publishing Company, p. 150; and T. Morrison and W. A. Conaway (2007). *Kiss, Bow, or Shake Hands: Latin America*. Avon, MA: F+W Publications, Inc., p. 47.

[22] Most of these visits involved business with several clients.

A07-14-0001

Appendix A. Telemedicine Diagnostic Devices and Software Defined

- **General Exam Camera:** Handheld or stationary high-definition examination camera that captures clear digital medical images and video files for multiple uses.
- **Stethoscope:** A medical instrument for detecting sounds produced in the body and transmitting them to the ears of a clinician through flexible tubing connected to a solid device placed upon the examined area.
- **Vital Signs Monitor/Pulse Oximeter:** A device for measuring the oxygen saturation of arterial blood by utilizing a sensor attached typically to a finger, toe, or ear.
- **Spirometer:** An instrument for measuring the air entering and leaving the lungs.
- **Ophthalmoscope:** An instrument for viewing the interior of the eye. Consists of a concave mirror with a hole in the center through which the observer examines the eye.
- **Otoscope:** An instrument fitted with lighting and magnifying lens systems used to facilitate visual examination of the auditory canal and eardrum.
- **Ultrasound Device:** A device that uses sound waves to form two-dimensional images used for the examination and measurement of internal body structures.
- **EKG Monitor:** A device that assesses electrical activity in the heart. An EKG Monitor translates the heart's electrical activity into line tracings on paper or a computer monitor.
- **CapSure®:** GlobalMed's DICOM-compliant medical imaging software that supports the acquisition, storage, and forwarding of high-quality high-definition medical images. Connected to CapSure Cloud®, GlobalMed's own cloud-based PACS (picture archiving and sharing system server), and to cloud-based third-party PACS servers, the software allows remote clinicians secure access to images.
- **CapSure® Cloud:** GlobalMed's cloud-based DICOM PACS, which supports camera images (both visible-light images), as well as Computed Tomography (CT), Magnetic Resonance (MRI), X-ray (CR), and Ultrasound (nonvisible light images).
- **eNcounter™:** GlobalMed's icon-based user-friendly interface application software, designed to provide a secure, configurable environment that protects personal information and blocks unauthorized changes. The software allows clinicians to initiate numerous types of configured applications (e.g., exam cameras, ultrasound, EKG, and others).

Sources: Accessed 19 November 2013 from the following:
    http://www.merriam-webster.com/medical/
    http://www.globalmed.com/products/peripherals.php
    http://www.webmd.com
